Phonics Bug

Teaching and Assessment Guide

Interactive synthetic phonics for reading and spelling

Reception (P1)

Joyce Watson & Rhona Johnston

Contents

Welcome to *Phonics Bug* 3

Teaching synthetic phonics using *Phonics Bug* 4

Phonics Bug Teaching Software navigation and controls 9

Guided independent work 15

Phonics Bug decodable readers 18

Phonics Bug eBooks and *Bug Club* 19

Phonics Bug components 20

Bug Club components 22

Assessing progress 24
- Before starting 24
- Assessment 26
- Assessment sheets 29
- Assessment and catch-up work in preparation for Key Stage 1 37
- What's next? 39

Guide to teaching Sessions 40

Daily lesson plans 43

Alphabetic overlay 107

About the authors 108

Welcome to Phonics Bug

Overview

Assess
Assess children's knowledge and understanding using the assessments in the *Phonics Bug Teaching and Assessment Guides* and the online tools. Keep the children in the whole-class teaching programme, and provide extra catch-up for the slower learners. Use the *Phonics Bug Prepare and Assess Handbook* and online resources to prepare children for the Phonics Screening Check in Year 1.

Teach
Teach whole-class phonics using the *Phonics Bug* teaching software and lesson plans for each Unit. Make use of the opportunities that whole-class teaching provides for ongoing observational assessment.

Practise
Consolidate pupils' understanding using the *Phonics Bug* PCMs and games, which can be found in the *Phonics Bug* teaching software.

Apply
Allocate the decodable readers and eBooks, matched to each Unit, to help pupils practise reading, ensuring that they approach any unfamiliar words by using their knowledge of phonics to decode the word. Extra breadth and variety is provided by the *Bug Club* books and eBooks.

Phonics Bug is the dedicated phonics strand of *Bug Club*, a core reading programme that can be used for independent and guided reading from Reception (Primary 1) to Year 6 (Primary 7). Together, *Phonics Bug* and *Bug Club* provide a complete solution to helping you teach children to read in Reception (P1) and Key Stage 1 (P2 and 3).

This Teaching and Assessment Guide focuses on *Phonics Bug*. The programme is a balanced approach to the teaching of reading using synthetic phonics (see page 4 for details). It simultaneously teaches the segmentation of words for spelling, and develops phonemic awareness skills. The programme is the product of seven years' research in Clackmannanshire, Scotland, which produced remarkable gains in reading and spelling among those children who followed the programme (the full research details are available within the software).

This interactive edition of the programme unites the proven pedagogy of the original programme with the most engaging and motivating delivery methods. This edition comprises:

- Teaching and Assessment Guides for Reception (P1) and Key Stage 1 (P2 and 3)
- Flashcards
- Photocopy Masters
- 134 decodable readers
- 134 eBooks and activities, available on www.bugclub.co.uk
- Teaching software and pupil games, available on www.bugclub.co.uk

Phonics Bug Quick Start

1) Go to **Before starting the programme** (page 24) and check that your children are ready to begin the programme.
2) Open the software and read **Software navigation and controls** (page 9).
3) Read the **Guide to teaching Sessions** (page 40).
4) Start using the programme!

Essential tips

- The basic Revision and Lesson elements of the Teaching Sessions are essential and should be carried out at a brisk pace. This may not be possible to begin with but, as you and your children get used to the format, the pace will quicken. The independent work provided by the PCMs and games can then be tailored to meet the needs of individuals or groups.
- Ideally the Sessions should be delivered on consecutive days, and if this is achieved, Units 1–12 will take around 16 weeks to complete. Teachers may decide to take a break between Units however.
- You will need an interactive whiteboard, but if you do not have access to one, simply use the Flashcards and make sure you have a large magnetic letter board and letters for modelling. (The Flashcards are available as printed items and are also downloadable from the software. They include picture stimuli, letters, words and sentences.)
- Your class will need small magnetic letter boards and letters for individual use or to share between two, as your professional judgement dictates.

Teaching synthetic phonics using *Phonics Bug*

What is synthetic phonics?

In synthetic phonics the graphemes and corresponding phonemes are taught just before the introduction of words that contain these letters. To read these words, children are taught to pronounce the individual phonemes (sounds) associated with the graphemes (letters) they see, and then to blend them together (synthesise) to form the word. (In this programme, we use slashes / / to denote phonemes and inverted commas ' ' to denote graphemes.) The process is as follows:

- Children *see* a word, e.g. "cat"; it is not pronounced for them.
- They break it down into its individual letters (graphemes) and pronounce the corresponding sounds (phonemes) for each letter in turn: /c/ /a/ /t/
- Then they blend the separate phonemes together to form the word.

This process is known as **blending**. (See page 46 for more details.)

Synthetic phonics teaches letter sounds very rapidly, explicitly showing children how to build up words with letters from the start, and always includes blending with printed words.

Synthetic phonics does not normally teach spelling, but *Phonics Bug* does teach spelling by reversing the reading process described above, i.e.

- Children *hear* a word, e.g. "cat" and say it.
- They say the first phoneme: /c/
- They write the corresponding grapheme: 'c'.
- They say the word again and say the next phoneme: /a/
- They write the corresponding grapheme: 'a', and so on.

This process is known as **segmenting**, and is followed by the children reading the word they have produced by sounding and blending.

In our approach, both blending for reading and segmenting for spelling are fully scaffolded. We model for the children how to sound and blend words for reading, but in each lesson children must attempt to sound and blend words for themselves to find out how they are pronounced. We also model for the children how to segment for spelling and continue to scaffold the children through the process with each word they spell. This ensures that they identify each phoneme and choose the appropriate grapheme in turn, until the word is spelt.

Synthetic phonics differs from analytic phonics in that in analytic phonics children are shown word families. For example, they may be introduced to the letter sound 'c', and then be shown a list of words all starting with the same letter sound, e.g. 'cat, cake, cut, cup'. Sounding and blending starts when all the letters of the alphabet have been taught in the beginning, middle and final positions of words, whereas in synthetic phonics this process starts after the first few letter sounds have been taught.

Programme rationale

Pace and order of teaching

In Reception, *Phonics Bug* teaches a new grapheme and related phoneme in every Phoneme Session. This fast pace, backed up by daily revision of past teaching, has proved the most effective and successful method of phonic training. This means that the basic 40+ phonemes are acquired quickly, and early reading skills develop rapidly. Decodable readers are introduced after just 10 days' teaching at the end of Unit 2. This enables children to apply the taught strategies and enjoy contextualised reading early on.

The order of grapheme introduction (see page 6) matches that recommended by the DfES in *Letters and Sounds* (2007) and ensures that children are able to start reading and spelling a wide range of words at the earliest possible stage.

Introduction of graphemes and phonemes

In *Phonics Bug* children are taught graphemes and phonemes at the same time. The research study showed that children progressed quickly if they learnt about phonemes in the context of letters and print right from the start of the phonics teaching.

Blending and segmenting

In *Phonics Bug* blending for reading and segmenting for spelling are given equal prominence, though blending is always taught first in a Session.

The practice of oral blending and segmentation is recommended in Phase 2 (see page 6 for more information on these 'Phases'). We suggest that these activities be done outside the lesson; for example, when there are a few minutes before the bell goes. Activities might include:

- suggesting words for children to practise sound-talk: e.g. tap, hat, mop
- using pictures from the online asset bank for sound-talk sentences, e.g.
    - Point to the m-a-p.
    - Can you h-o-p on one l-e-g?

Introduction of letter names

The names of letters can be taught first, via the Alphabet song and magnetic letters. During the seven or so years over which the programme has been in use, children have not had any difficulties learning both letter names and sounds early on. One of the benefits of this is that any child who misses a Session will know the names of the letters they have missed. In many cases the letter names give a good guide to the letter sounds. However, the teaching of letter names is optional in this programme.

Teaching synthetic phonics using *Phonics Bug*

Multi-sensory learning

Bringing a multi-sensory element to the teaching of phonics is widely recognised to be hugely beneficial to its effectiveness. *Phonics Bug* recommends the use of magnetic letters and boards to consolidate children's blending and segmenting abilities. Mini-magnetic boards are to be used by pairs (or individuals) during and after the Whole-Class Teaching Sessions. The interactive whiteboard acts as an electronic magnetic letter board for teacher demonstration.

Additionally, teaching the formation of the letters at the same time as the sounds helps to consolidate the letters in memory. Once children are competent at writing the letters, they need not use the individual boards for spelling.

Handwriting

Phonics Bug does not necessarily seek to replace your normal handwriting programme, but it does recognise that letter formation helps kinaesthetic consolidation of grapheme acquisition and so spelling. The teaching of letter formation accompanies the introduction of every grapheme and the talking-through element of such teaching also supports the children's cognitive processes.

Note: The letter formation is non-cursive, so if you teach cursive handwriting, you may wish to omit this feature from your lessons and deal with handwriting separately.

Less common grapheme–phoneme correspondences

Based on experience of the hundreds of children who have been through the programme over the last ten or so years, *Phonics Bug* takes the view that children are best served by learning the basic 40+ grapheme–phoneme correspondences in the first year at school. The less frequent pronunciations, particularly for vowels, are taught when the children are secure in the basic principles, normally in the second year of school (see page 19).

Very minor variations in pronunciation are not taught separately, and this has been found to pose no relevant difficulties for the children. We do, however, provide special notes within daily lesson plans, which outline areas where you may want to adopt your own regional pronunciation.

High frequency (common) words and irregular words

High frequency decodable common words are included for reading and spelling throughout *Phonics Bug*. These are listed in the chart under 'Decodable words' and are always taught by sounding and blending. There is also a list of 'Not fully decodable (irregular) words'; the term used in *Letters and Sounds* is 'tricky words'. These words are subsumed under the heading 'Irregular' in the Language Sessions (see below). Many of these words have spellings that have irregular pronunciations; these words are always deemed 'tricky', e.g. 'one'. However, some of the words in the list have regular pronunciations and become fully decodable later on as the phonics teaching progresses; for example, 'like' becomes completely decodable when split digraphs are taught.

Children are encouraged to use their phonic knowledge to help them decode these words as far as possible; you can point out and talk through the irregular aspects to help them read the words. (See page 52 for more details of how to do this.) You may want to introduce additional irregular words as deemed necessary by the content of your particular reading schemes. You may also want to practise the irregular words throughout the school day. However, these words, and the high frequency decodable words, are never taught as 'sight' words using flash cards.

The following chart shows the *Phonics Bug* progression in common words (decodable and not fully decodable) in Reception (Primary 1).

Phase	Unit	Decodable words	No-fully decodable words (Irregular words)
2	1	at, as	
	2	an, it, in, is, dad	
	3	can, on, not, got	to
	4	mum, up, get	the, no, go
	5	had, back, his, big, him, if, of, off, but	I, into
3	6	will	me, be
	7	–	he, my, by
	8	that, this, then, them, with	they, she
	9	look, see, too	we, are
	10	for, now, down	you, her
	11	–	all, was
4	12	went, from, children, just, help	said, have, like, so, do, some, come, were, there, little, one, when, out, what

Language Sessions

Language Sessions occur at the end of each Unit. These Sessions combine the teaching of irregular words with using words in the context of captions and sentences. The acquisition of skills for reading single words is only part of the reading process. To read with fluency and comprehension, children need to apply and develop the skills taught during the synthetic phonics teaching element of the programme. The Language Sessions serve to consolidate the teaching of reading and spelling in the Phoneme Sessions, and promote early comprehension skills.

Comprehension is not an end product. It is a process which occurs during active interaction between the reader and the text. In the *Phonics Bug* Language Sessions, a progressive programme of text-related directed activities has been assembled to enable children to progress from single-word reading to reading intelligently to grasp meaning from the text.

While there are no new grapheme–phoneme correspondences in Phase 4, it is important that children learn to read and spell words containing adjacent consonants and read more decodable words and words that are not fully decodable (irregular words). For this reason there are three (rather than one) Language Sessions in Unit 12 (Phase 4).

Teaching synthetic phonics using *Phonics Bug*

Guided independent work

Although *Phonics Bug* is delivered through teacher-modelling and rehearsal with the whole class, there are also resources for guided independent work. These can be tailored to meet the needs of an individual or groups and to give you a chance to work with children who may need more help to consolidate their learning. The resources consist of one photocopy master (PCM) for each Session, plus up to five pupil games per Unit that can start to be used after the end of each Unit.

Introduction of graded readers

Phonics Bug is supported by decodable readers which match the order of phoneme introduction.

When the children have completed the first two Units of *Phonics Bug*, they will have acquired a sufficient number of grapheme–phoneme correspondences to start reading their own books. This should be a motivating and enjoyable experience for them.

There are books to match each Unit of the teaching programme and these help children to practise and consolidate their learning at each stage.

Before, during and after the introduction of the *Phonics Bug* readers, children should be exposed constantly to a rich and varied diet of book experiences to ensure their enthusiasm for reading is nurtured, their comprehension skills are being developed, and their speaking and listening skills are extended.

Speaking and listening skills

Our strategy of teacher-modelling and rehearsal for teaching reading and spelling provides opportunities for pupils to be both spectators and participants. As spectators, they listen to words and structures; as participants, they try them out. While sharing pupil magnetic boards, working in pairs or small groups, pupils respond to each other, learning to adjust the language to suit the situation and the response of partners. Using graded readers, the teacher can encourage pupils to express opinions and explore, develop and sustain ideas through talk and discussion.

Teaching sequence

Phonics Bug is structured with Phoneme Sessions and Language Sessions (see page 7 for the breakdown of the 'Teaching Elements' in both these Session types). The following diagram illustrates the alignment of the *Phonics Bug* lesson structure to the recommended teaching sequence.

Recommended Teaching Sequence	*Phonics Bug* Lesson Structure
Introduce ▼	Learning intentions and outcomes for the day are discussed at the start of the lesson. The daily lesson plans in this guide provide an overview of these learning intentions/outcomes.
Revisit and Review ▼	Every Phoneme Session begins with Revision to review previous learning (with the exception of Unit 1). In Reception (P1) the Revision is not just of the previous day's target grapheme-phoneme correspondence, but also of blending for reading and segmenting for spelling of the relevant words. In Key Stage 1 (P2&3) the Revision is sometimes a review of previous learning which links with the planned teaching for that day.
Teach ▼	Every Phoneme and Language Session is composed of Teaching Elements (e.g. Sounds, Reading, Spelling etc) which are easily navigated to structure the new phonic teaching. The teaching of grapheme-phoneme correspondences and high-frequency (common) words is covered.
Practise ▼	Practise opportunities are available in the following areas: • 'Follow-up' parts of the lessons • Unit-linked pupil games • Unit-linked photocopy masters • 'Free-teaching' within the software's Magnetic Board
Apply ▼	Language Sessions provide opportunities to apply developing phonic skills to the reading, spelling and writing of captions and sentences. This application also covers Irregular (not fully decodable) common words. In addition the linked decodable readers allow regular application of children's phonic skills, from as early as Unit 2 of *Phonics Bug*.
Assess Learning	Assessment guidance and materials provided within this guide and in the software enable ongoing formative assessment during the daily lessons and summative assessment at regular periods through the programme. The *Phonics Bug Prepare and Assess Handbook* and online resources can be used to prepare children for the Phonics Screening Check in Year 1.

Teaching synthetic phonics using *Phonics Bug*

Programme structure

Unit structure

The following table shows what is covered in each of Units 1–12 of *Phonics Bug* and relates the content to the 'Phases' of progression recommended by the DfE document *Letters and Sounds*. (See also the section '*Phonics Bug* and the Phases of Progression' on page 8.) The Unit structure of *Phonics Bug* also matches exactly the phoneme order recommended by the DfES in *Letters and Sounds* (2007).

- Each of the 12 Units represents a group of letters.
- Each phoneme within a group is introduced in one Phoneme Session, and each Unit concludes with a Language Session, which includes the teaching of associated irregular words.

Phase	Unit	Focus	Not fully decodable/ Irregular words
2	1	s a t p	
	2	i n m d	
	3	g o c k	to
	4	ck e u r	the, no, go
	5	h b f, ff l, ll ss	I, into
3	6	j v w x	me, be
	7	y z, zz qu	he, my, by
	8	ch sh th ng	they, she
	9	ai ee igh oa oo (long) oo (short)	we, are
	10	ar or ur ow oi	you, her
	11	ear air ure er	all, was
4	12	Adjacent consonants (cvcc, ccvc, ccvcc, cccvc, cccvcc)	said, have, like, so, do, some, come, were, there, little, one, when, out, what

(See page 39 for a table showing what is covered in each of Units 13–30 of *Phonics Bug*.)

Session structure

The following table illustrates the breakdown of Teaching Elements in Phoneme and Language Sessions.

- Every Phoneme and Language Session is composed of the same Teaching Elements (with the exception of Unit 1).
- Each Phoneme Session starts with Revision to review previous learning (with the exception of Unit 1).
- Each Lesson within the Phoneme Session starts by introducing the new phoneme for the day, sometimes using a fun video clip. Children examine Asset bank words in order to highlight the new grapheme in beginning, middle or end positions. It is not intended that children read these words out loud.

Phoneme Session

Teaching Element	Description
Alphabet song	Sing the Alphabet song
Revision	
Letters and Sounds	Quick-fire practice of previously taught grapheme-phoneme correspondences
Reading	Children practise reading words composed of previously taught grapheme-phoneme correspondences
Writing and Spelling	Children practise spelling and letter formation using previously taught graphemes and words
Lesson	
Introduction	Discuss learning intentions and outcomes for the day
Sounds	Children are introduced to new grapheme with corresponding phoneme. They highlight the letter's position in words from the Asset bank
Reading	Children blend phonemes for reading words
Spelling	Children segment words for spelling
Writing	Children form letters to cement grapheme-phoneme correspondence
Follow-up	Children are introduced to guided independent work, consolidating any teaching from Lesson
Plenary	Discuss learning outcomes
Alphabet song	Sing the Alphabet song

Language Session

Teaching Element	Description
Alphabet song	Sing the Alphabet song
Introduction	Discuss learning intentions and outcomes for the day
Not fully decodable words/Irregular words	
Reading	Children read irregular word(s)
Spelling	Children spell irregular word(s)
Lesson	
Reading	Children read captions and sentences
Spelling	Children spell captions and sentences
Writing	Children write captions and sentences
Follow-up	Basic comprehension and introduction of guided independent work
Plenary	Discuss learning outcomes
Alphabet song	Sing the Alphabet song

Teaching synthetic phonics using *Phonics Bug*

Phonics Bug and the Phases of Progression

Phonics Bug provides inbuilt formative and summative assessment that follows closely the phonics phases outlined in *Letters and Sounds*. The letter order used in this programme follows that recommended in *Letters and Sounds*, following a sequence that early on makes the reading of a large number of CVC words possible. Knowledge of the Phase 2 and 3 letters, digraphs and trigraphs can be tested using Assessments 1 to 4, and the ability to read and spell CVC non-words can be measured using Assessment 5. However, you should not expect the children to have mastery of what they have been taught right at the end of each Phase. During the Clackmannanshire study, children at the end of Phase 3 only got about 50% of these non-words correct; yet when tested a year later only 2.2% of the children were more than a year behind in reading, and none was more than 2 years behind. Phase 4 skills (adjacent consonants) are assessed in Assessment 6, where children are asked to read and spell CCVC, CVCC and CCVCC non-words. Advice on how to support struggling learners can be found on pages 37 and 38; these children should do extra catch-up sessions while staying in the whole-class programme.

A fun, informal group assessment of words and non-words is available in the *Phonics Bug Prepare and Assess* online word generator tool, whilst formal photocopiable tests are available in the *Prepare and Assess Handbook*. These tests are designed specifically to help you to prepare children for the Government's Phonics Screening Check in Year 1.

How to run the programme

Duration of programme

Units 1–12 support the suggested timetable for teaching Phases 2, 3 and 4 within the first year of school – for example, teaching four letters per week in Phase 2. The Units can take as little as 16 weeks to complete, but you should of course use your professional judgement to moderate the pace in accordance with the needs of the class. You may, for example, want to break for a week or so after you have finished introducing the single-letter phonemes, and use this time for assessment and catching up.

It is envisaged that the Sessions will be delivered on consecutive days. This will not always be possible or sensible, but you should try to maintain the brisk pace of lesson delivery as far as possible in order to achieve maximum benefits from the programme.

It should be noted that it is not expected that all of the children will have complete mastery of the phonemes as they are taught. The children will be able to master them in subsequent sessions, as they come up over and over again.

Daily time allocation

The time it takes to deliver the whole-class Sessions will depend on your familiarity with the programme and how you choose to use the more flexible elements such as the video clips, alphabet song and so on. The independent work provided by the PCMs does not necessarily have to be done immediately after the Whole-Class Session, but it should be completed before the next Session if possible. The games can be used as consolidation work at any point in the day, and are ideal for slower learners if appropriate to their learning needs. You will notice that Unit 1 contains less content than the other Units, but it is still recommended to use your full time allocation for these Sessions as the children will need more support when first introduced to the programme.

Classroom organisation

It is recommended that the children are kept together for the Daily Sessions in spite of different ability levels. This has been shown to foster a sense of social inclusion and boost the performance of the children who are progressing more slowly. However, you will need to differentiate your questioning within the lesson to ensure that all children are fully engaged. Some of the follow-up activities are provided at different levels to help support different ability levels. See page 37 for further information on how to form a nurture/needs group for slower learners.

Children usually sit together on the floor in front of the interactive whiteboard at the start of the daily Teaching Sessions for the Introduction, Revision, Lesson Sounds, Lesson Visual Search and Lesson Reading elements. The children return to their seats when the Spelling element is reached.

Classroom management of the magnetic letters

The children should be provided with small magnetic letter boards and appropriate sets of magnetic letters (e.g. for Unit 1, s, a, t, p plus one or two distractors). One board between two is ideal. Paired work is useful because it enables the children to explain what they are doing and hear explanations from others, and in so doing consolidate the learning. (Additional magnetic letters will be required when double letters are being practised.)

The boards should be available on the children's tables, and the children should return to their seats when the Spelling Teaching Element is reached during the Daily Phoneme Session to build the target words themselves on their boards. As children become more advanced they will begin to spell using pencil and paper instead of magnetic letters.

You may find it useful to place the photocopiable alphabetic overlay provided in this guide (page 107) on top of each of the boards. The magnetic letters should be placed in their correct positions on the overlay at the end of each Session, thereby consolidating knowledge of the alphabet and making it easier to see if any letters are missing.

Phonics Bug Teaching Software navigation and controls

The *Phonics Bug* teaching software is accessed from www.bugclub.co.uk. Simply go to the website, enter your personal log-in details and click on the Phonics Software tab. From here you will be able to launch the software for display on your whiteboard. (You can also access the eBooks from this website, see page 19 for more details.)

Main Menu

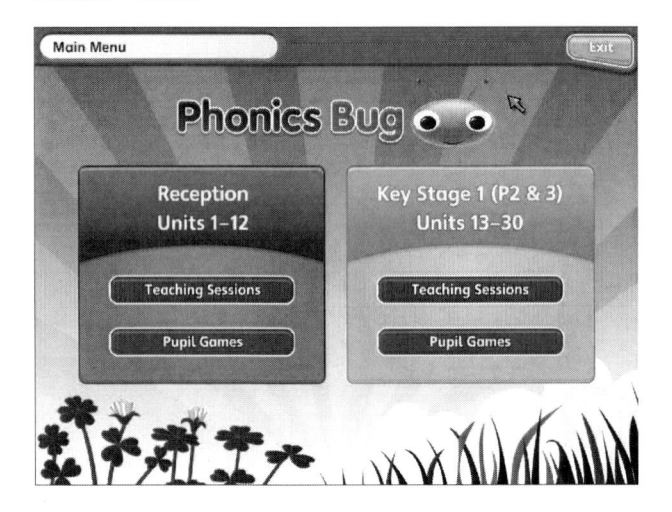

On starting the software you will be presented with the Main Menu as shown above left. Choose which part of the programme (Units 1–12 or Units 13–30) you wish to enter from this Main Menu.

You will now be presented with a screen containing the Unit and Session Select Menu, as shown above right. The function of this menu is described below. The Navigation bar at the top of the screen contains four buttons. The 'Tour' button contains an on-screen tour that demonstrates how to use the main features of the software. Clicking 'Help' will take you to the relevant help areas. Clicking 'Back' will take you back to the Main Menu, and clicking 'Exit' will enable you to leave the software. At the bottom of the screen are some Additional features. These provide links to the 'Pupil Games', 'Print Material' and 'Magnetic Board'. These features are described in more detail later on.

Unit and Session Select Menu

When you select a Unit from the Unit Select menu, the Session Select menu will become populated. There are two kinds of Sessions within each Unit: Phoneme Sessions and Language Sessions.

If you select a Phoneme Session, the Revision and Lesson buttons will appear, as shown below left.

If you select a Language Session, the Irregular and Lesson buttons will appear, as seen below right. Clicking on any of these buttons will take you into the main body of the software.

Please note: Some early Units do not have any Revision, Language or Irregular content, and Unit 12 has 3 Language Sessions.

Phonics Bug Teaching Software navigation and controls

Controls

Diagram labels: Navigation bar, Teaching Element Tabs, Toolbar, Work area, Guide character, Alphabet panel

On reaching the main body of the software, you will be presented with a similar screen to the one shown above. There are a number of controls on this screen that are important for getting the most out of your software.

When you enter the screen for the first time, a pop-up will appear, describing how to use the controls on the screen. Clicking 'Do not show this again' will ensure that this guide will not reappear. You can, however, access it at any time by clicking on the Guide button on the Navigation bar.

Work area

The light blue area in the middle of the screen is called the Work area. This is where the Session takes place.

Guide character

The Guide character has been programmed to give the children encouragement and feedback. Clicking directly on the Guide character will pause the animation; clicking again will resume playback.

Teaching Elements

Each Session is broken down into a number of Teaching Elements. These are accessed by clicking on the Tabs at the top of the Work area:

Tabs: Sounds | Reading | Spelling | Writing | Follow-up

Navigation bar

Navigation bar: Phonics Bug | Unit 3 Phoneme o: Lesson | Guide | Back | Exit

The Navigation bar contains three buttons as shown above. Clicking 'Back' will return you to the Unit and Session Select Menu, and clicking 'Exit' will enable you to leave the software. Clicking 'Guide' will open a dialog box that contains the teaching points for the Teaching Element that you are currently on.

Phonics Bug Teaching Software navigation and controls

Toolbar

The Toolbar sits down the left-hand side of the screen.

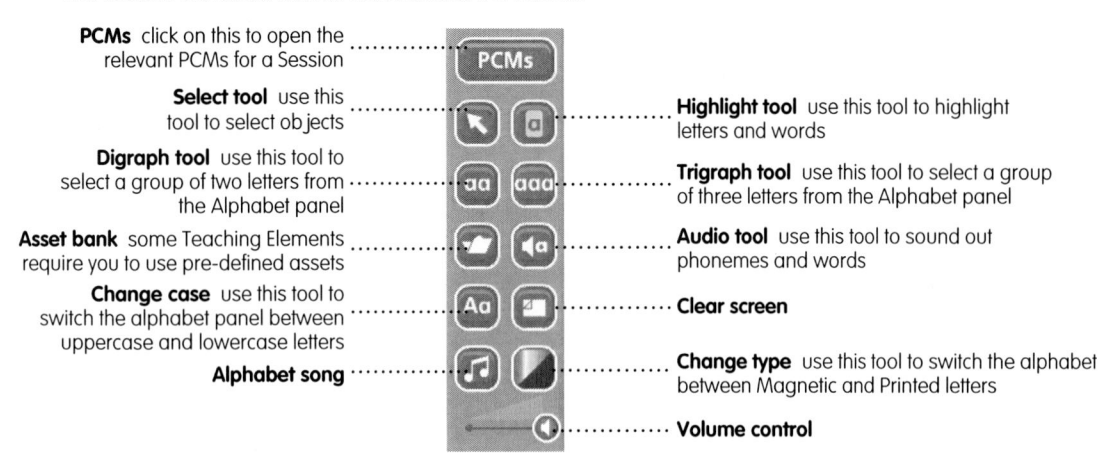

PCMs click on this to open the relevant PCMs for a Session

Select tool use this tool to select objects

Digraph tool use this tool to select a group of two letters from the Alphabet panel

Asset bank some Teaching Elements require you to use pre-defined assets

Change case use this tool to switch the alphabet panel between uppercase and lowercase letters

Alphabet song

Highlight tool use this tool to highlight letters and words

Trigraph tool use this tool to select a group of three letters from the Alphabet panel

Audio tool use this tool to sound out phonemes and words

Clear screen

Change type use this tool to switch the alphabet between Magnetic and Printed letters

Volume control

Alphabet song

The Alphabet song has three buttons, sitting at the top right of the screen.

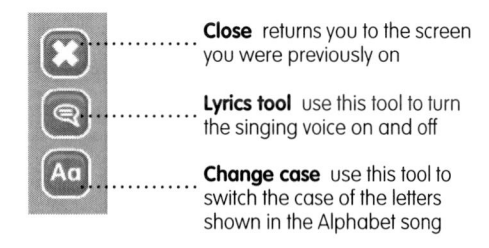

Close returns you to the screen you were previously on

Lyrics tool use this tool to turn the singing voice on and off

Change case use this tool to switch the case of the letters shown in the Alphabet song

Alphabet panel

Bin

a b c d e f g h i j k l m n o p q r s t u v w x y z

At the bottom of the screen is the Alphabet panel. This has been positioned specifically so that it is within reach of the children. Letters from the Alphabet panel can be moved onto the Work area either by clicking and dragging them, or simply by clicking once. The Teaching Element that you are currently on determines where the letters can be dropped onto the Work area. Letters can be removed from the Work area by dragging them into the Bin (see above) or by clicking the Clear screen button on the Toolbar (see top of this page).

Control panel

Scroll through content

Eye

Control buttons

Some Teaching Elements are managed by a Control panel that sits at the top right of the Work area. This Control panel is tailored to the Teaching Element that you are currently on, and the Control buttons on the right-hand side will alter accordingly.

Clicking on the arrows will allow you to scroll through the pre-defined content for the current Teaching Element. Clicking on the Eye will allow you to preview the content.

Phonics Bug Teaching Software navigation and controls

Video

Some Teaching Elements contain a video clip. The tools from the Toolbar are still available for you to use during the playing of the video.

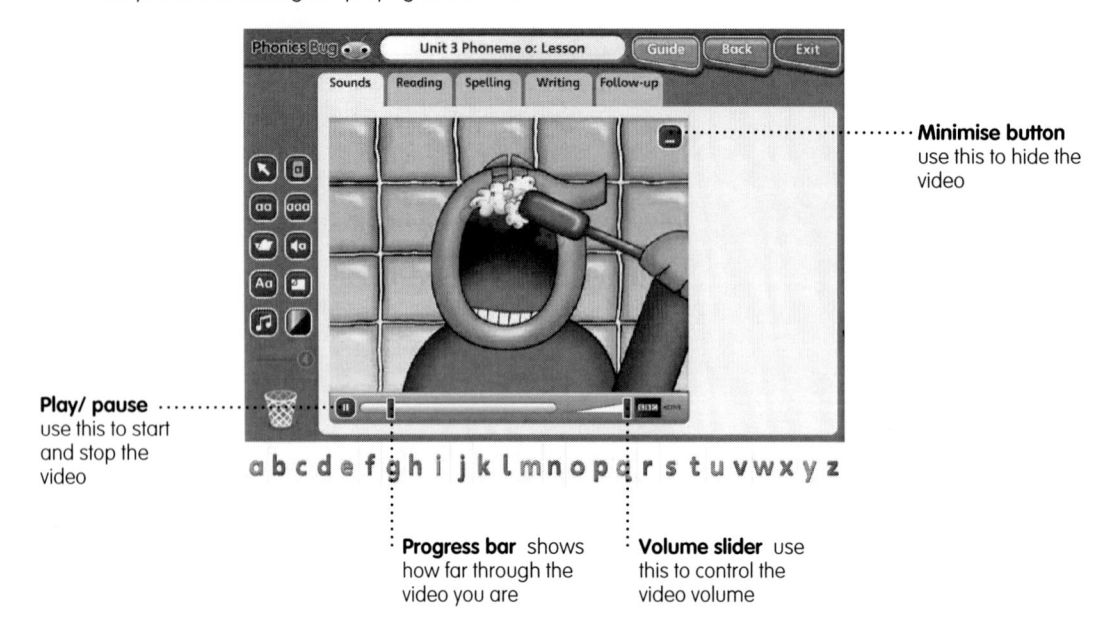

Minimise button use this to hide the video

Play/ pause use this to start and stop the video

Progress bar shows how far through the video you are

Volume slider use this to control the video volume

Phonics Bug Teaching Software navigation and controls

Pupil Games

Unit and Game Select menu

Clicking on 'Pupil Games' from the Unit and Session Select Menu will bring you to the screen above. There are five different games for the pupils to play: Sounds, Names, Reading, Spelling, Language. There is a version of each game for every Unit apart from Unit 1. On entering this screen you will be presented with the Unit and Game Select Menu. This operates in the same manner as the Unit and Session Select Menu. To begin a game, simply click 'Start'.

Score panel

Play area

Control panel

Each Pupil Game has a similar interface. The Pupil Games are very easy to use and the instructions are explained before the game starts. The instructions can also be accessed by clicking 'Guide' on the Navigation bar or found on pages 16–17 of this Teaching Guide.

Each game has a Play area where the action happens, a Score panel and a Control panel.

Phonics Bug Teaching Software navigation and controls

Print Material

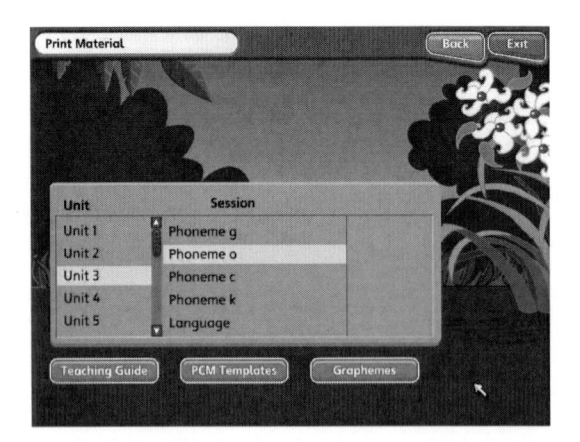

Clicking on 'Print Material' on the Unit and Session Select Menu will bring you to the screen above. There are two different kinds of print material specific to each Unit and Session: the PCMs and the Resources, both supplied as PDFs. The PCMs are copies of those printed in the *Phonics Bug Photocopy Masters* book and the Resources can be printed out and made into cards.

In addition to the print material specific to each Unit and Session, you will find PDF print material specific to each assessment and catch-up activity for Units 1–12 (the PCM Assessment sheets in this Teaching Guide and Flashcard Resources).

At the bottom of the screen there are three additional features. Clicking 'Teaching Guide' will open a PDF of this document and clicking 'Graphemes' will open a document, again, which can be printed out and made into cards.

Phonics Bug also contains additional resources allowing you to create your own PCMs for independent use. These consist of PCM Templates in the form of Word documents and a selection of clipart, which can be accessed by clicking on 'PCM Templates' at the bottom of the screen. A Zip file will be downloaded to a location specified by you. This Zip file can be extracted by double-clicking on it and following the on-screen instructions. In order to use the clipart simply open one of the Templates in Microsoft Word and select 'Insert', 'Picture' and 'From file' from the menu at the top of the screen and then point to the location of the extracted clipart.

Magnetic Board

The Magnetic Board is the final feature accessible from the Unit and Session Select Menu. This is a blank screen that can be used to continue your teaching of phonics, outside of the *Phonics Bug* lesson structure. Furthermore, the Asset bank accessible from this screen allows you access to all the assets (pictures, words and sentences) from Units 1–12.

Note: The multi-coloured magnetic letters of the alphabet can be switched to printed letters of the same colour by clicking the 'Change type' button. Clicking on the 'Change case' button switches the alphabet between lowercase and uppercase letters.

Guided independent work

Photocopy masters (PCMs)

Over 60 PCMs have been specifically written for independent consolidation work, to be completed once you have modelled and rehearsed the Teaching Elements in the Whole-Class Session. They don't necessarily need to be completed immediately after the Whole-Class Session but should be done before the next Session. There are two types of PCM provided to accompany the teaching of *Phonics Bug*:

Phoneme Session PCM

To be completed after each Phoneme Session, each of these PCMs consolidates the three areas covered in the Lesson: matching graphemes to their alphabetic positions, identifying graphemes in different positions in words, and letter formation.

Language Session PCM

To be completed after each Language Session, each of these PCMs comprises two tasks which aim to consolidate the children's comprehension skills. You will find that some of these tasks mirror the software's Language Session follow-up Teaching Elements. The table below charts the progression of tasks covered in the Language Session PCMs.

Instructional text

Each task is preceded by a printed instruction. You may read this with the whole class, and perhaps draw attention to certain phrases such as 'Put a ring around …', 'Write the letter …', 'Look at the picture …' and 'Read the sentence …'. Please bear in mind that the children are by no means expected to read these instructions at the beginning stage of the programme, but it is hoped that, with time, they will become familiar with these words, understand their meanings and begin to read the instructions themselves.

Differentiated tasks

The phoneme PCMs are not differentiated but, for children who are struggling with the letter formation task, you may decide to leave the formation of some of the uppercase letters until later on.

In Units 5–11, there are two differentiated versions of the Language Session PCMs to cater for different ability groups. In the tasks where the children are required to write out words, one version of the PCMs provides short blank lines to prompt the children as to the number of letters in each target word, while the other version does not provide such prompts; in this latter case the children will write the whole word on one line.

Self-assessment

At the bottom of each PCM you will see 'happy' and 'sad' faces. In order to encourage children to consider their own performance, they should tick one of the faces in accordance with how confident they felt about the tasks. In the first half of the programme, each PCM contains only the 'happy' and 'sad' faces. From Unit 8 onwards, when the tasks become more complicated, the children are given an additional 'neutral' face to choose from, to encourage them to think about the finer distinctions between being simply satisfied or dissatisfied with their performances. For example, they may select the 'neutral' face if they feel that they have performed particularly well in one task but not the other.

Language PCM task progression

Task / Units	2	3	4	5	6	7	8	9	10	11	12(i)	12(ii)	12(iii)
Matching words to words	●												
Matching pictures to words	●	●	●										
Drawing pictures for captions		●	●	●									
Writing words for pictures				●									
Drawing pictures for sentences					●	●							
Writing sentences for pictures							●	●	●	●			
Cloze procedures with picture clues					●	●	●						
Cloze procedures with word clues								●	●	●			
Selecting correct sentences											●	●	●
Complete story by writing its ending											●	●	
Complete story by writing its beginning													●

Guided independent work

Create your own PCMs

A number of Templates (including a clipart bank) have been provided on the software, allowing you to create your own PCMs to match your class's requirements (see page 14).

Pupil Games

There are five Pupil Games in each Unit (except Unit 1), each game consolidating one of the five areas that the children have been working on in the Lessons:

- Sounds
- Names
- Reading
- Spelling
- Language

Sounds

What is tested

This game tests the children's knowledge of the graphemes and their corresponding phonemes.

How to play

The children will hear a phoneme being read out, and have to find the corresponding grapheme from a selection of graphemes. If they select correctly, they will see a reward animation.

Score

There is a maximum of 10 points to be scored.

Names

What is tested

This game tests the children's knowledge of the letters of the alphabet and the letter names.

How to play

The children will hear a letter name being read out, and have to find the corresponding letter from a selection of letters. If they select correctly, they will see a reward animation.

Score

There is a maximum of 10 points to be scored.

Reading

What is tested

This game tests the children's ability to match the pronunciation of words to their spellings.

How to play

The children will hear a word being read out, and they have to find the correct word from a selection of words at the bottom of the screen. If they select correctly, they will see a reward animation.

Score

There is a maximum of 10 points to be scored.

Guided independent work

Spelling

What is tested
This game tests the children's ability to spell words.

How to play
The children will hear a word being read out, and they have to select the correct letters to spell the word by scrolling through a list of letters, using the up and down arrows by the character boxes. Once they have spelt the word, they click on 'OK'. If the word is spelt correctly, the children will see a reward animation.

Score
There is a maximum of 6 points to be scored.

Language

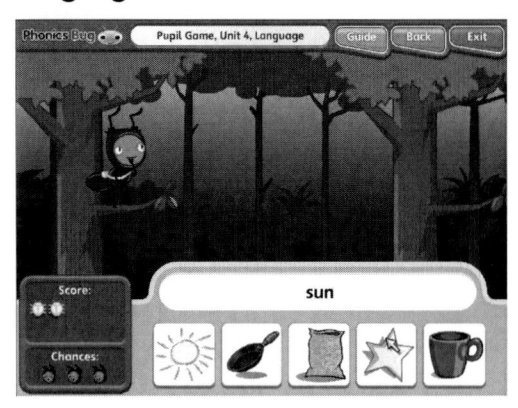

What is tested
This game tests the children's comprehension skills, by testing their ability to match captions and sentences with pictures, as well as their ability to fill in missing words to complete sentences.

How to play
There are 3 different levels to this game, reflecting to a strong degree the exercises in the PCMs:

- In Units 1–5, the children are required to select pictures that match the given captions.
- In Units 6–9, the children are required to select pictures that best relate to the captions and sentences.
- From Unit 10 onwards, the children are required to select pictures or words to complete the given sentences.

If they select correctly, they will see a reward animation.

Score
There is a maximum of 10 points to be scored.

Pupil Game task progression

Game	Task	Units	1	2	3	4	5	6	7	8	9	10	11	12
Sounds	Selecting graphemes for given phonemes			●	●	●	●	●	●	●	●	●	●	●
Names	Selecting letters for given letter names			●	●	●	●	●	●	●	●	●	●	●
Reading	Selecting words which are pronounced			●	●	●	●	●	●	●	●	●	●	●
Spelling	Spelling words which are pronounced			●	●	●	●	●	●	●	●	●	●	●
Language	Selecting pictures that match captions		●	●	●	●								
	Selecting pictures that best relate to given sentences							●	●	●	●	●	●	●
	Selecting appropriate words to complete the given sentences											●	●	●

Phonics Bug decodable readers

The *Phonics Bug* readers have been designed to fully support the teaching sessions in the *Phonics Bug* software and daily lesson plans. The books have been written to match the order in which grapheme-phoneme correspondences are introduced in *Phonics Bug* (and in *Letters and Sounds*). The books begin at Phase 2 and continue through to Phase 5.

Each Unit of *Phonics Bug* links with a series of decodable texts. These are designed to give children the opportunity to practise their blending skills and to consolidate their knowledge of grapheme-phoneme correspondences, in the context of engaging texts, in addition to the sentence level work on the Language Sessions.

Using the books

We are aware that the *Phonics Bug* readers may be used for a variety of purposes, such as Independent Reading, assessment, take-home reading and guided reading. Therefore, we have tried to make the teaching support (printed inside the covers of the books) as flexible as possible.

Decodability

The books have been designed to support children as they gain in confidence and become fluent and automatic decoders. The books do not contain any grapheme-phoneme correspondence until it has been taught in the main teaching programme, with the exception of a few common irregular ('tricky') words needed to make the text meaningful. The points at which these are introduced match to the Phases in which they are introduced in the teaching plans, although the Phase 3 books do contain a few words with adjacent consonants. Children should sound and blend unfamiliar words until they have sight recognition of them; they should not guess from context or use picture cues.

In Phase 5, we have followed the introduction of graphemes according to the order set out in the teaching software. However, in some instances, we have introduced additional graphemes (i.e. 'u' for long /oo/ in Set 18 and 'our' for /or/ in Set 19). Furthermore, there is one instance where we have introduced a grapheme slightly earlier than in the teaching plans. We have introduced the grapheme 'le' for /l/ in Set 24 to enable us to cover the 'st' grapheme for /s/ in this Set (for example, in words such as 'castle' and 'whistle').

Some books contain environmental print which is often above the reading level of the child. The adult can decide whether or not to draw attention to this text as appropriate.

Polysyllabic words

Simple polysyllabic words (words with two syllables or more) are introduced from Set 5. These words are pulled out and given special attention in the teaching notes when they occur. Children sometimes have problems with polysyllabic words as they have to break down the word into its component syllables, before blending each one and then combining them to read the whole word.

Plurals and 3rd person verbs

Simple plurals and 's' forms of verbs are used from the start as they are extremely common and research indicates that they do not pose problems for most children. These word forms are not referred to as adjacent consonants.

Sentence level progression

In addition to the cumulative coverage of grapheme-phoneme correspondences, *Phonics Bug* readers also develop their level of challenge in other ways. They gradually move from captions in the earliest books, through to simple sentences and more complex sentence structures in the later ones. There is also a carefully planned gradual increase in the number of words and the number of different words at each level. The stories themselves also become generally more sophisticated at later levels, while maintaining their appropriateness for the age group.

Book Bands

We have not attempted to place the *Phonics Bug* readers in Book Bands, as we recognise that the Book Band levelling system is designed for texts constructed on a very different basis from phonic readers. However, to help teachers organise their resources, a very rough correlation can be made:

Letters and Sounds Phase	Book Band
Phase 2	Pink
Phase 3	Red–Yellow
Phase 4	Yellow
Phase 5	Blue–Orange

Phonics Bug eBooks and Bug Club website

Using Phonics Bug and Bug Club readers together

The *Phonics Bug* readers are designed to support children in practising and consolidating the knowledge they acquire during the whole-class teaching sessions. They also allow children to experience the pleasure of reading their own books. In addition, children need to access a rich variety of books, so that they develop enthusiasm for reading. The books available in *Bug Club* are the perfect complement to *Phonics Bug*. They are aligned to the Phases of *Letters and Sounds*, and the chart on pages 22–23 shows the phonic progression within them. The books contain a small number of words that are classed as 'tricky' for a particular phonics level. This is so that the stories can be richer and more meaningful – and so that they can help children develop the vital skill of comprehension.

Teachers vary in their approach to organising resources. You might find it helpful to keep the decodable readers in a separate box, and use them specifically for consolidating phonics work. You could then use the *Bug Club* books for further consolidation and application of decoding skills, as well as comprehension. The *Phonics Bug* and *Bug Club* books are finely levelled to ensure that children feel that they are making progress. It is not necessary for every child to read every book, as some will progress faster than others, but the two series provide plenty of breadth and choice at each level, to help make sure that all children get the reading experiences they need to progress.

Phonics Bug eBooks and the Bug Club website

Once a child has read a *Phonics Bug* book, they can practise reading that text again, using the *Phonics Bug* eBooks which are accessed through a child's personalised online reading world. The eBooks have three main features for the child:

- **Phoneme pronunciation guide:** A child (and parent) can hear audio recordings of the sounds that each book is designed to practise, so that they can listen out for them during their reading.
- **Read to Me:** A child can also hear a model reading of the text. We recommend that you do not use this 'Read to Me' feature before the child has read the printed books for the first time, as the aim of synthetic phonics teaching is to enable pupils to work out the pronunciation of unfamiliar words for themselves. This feature can be used subsequently as a model of fluent reading, to help them give expression to their reading, and to develop a sense of how stories work.
- **Quiz question**: A child can read the text again onscreen, but this time, access an interactive quiz question embedded within the book pages. Each question is designed to reinforce phonic skills, and attempted questions feed back information to teachers.

Bug Club's online reading world

Bug Club's online reading world helps children improve core reading skills at school or home with exciting texts and fun rewards. It also enables teachers to monitor every child's progress, providing valuable evidence of their reading for Assessment Focus 1 in Assessing Pupils' Progress (APP). *Bug Club* contains 305 *Bug Club* books, as well as the 134 *Phonics Bug* books. *Bug Club* books have a greater range of quiz questions, designed to reinforce comprehension skills and provide information across the full range of the Assessment Focuses.

Child experience

Bug Club facilitates independent practice at school, home, or any computer that has an internet connection. With easy-to-remember logins (which you can also personalise) a child can log in to their personalised reading homepage and access eBooks for further reading practice.

My Books: Five eBooks can be allocated to a child at one time. Children can also re-read the last 10 eBooks again, and see how many eBooks they have read in total.

Bug Points and Rewards: A child can collect Bug Points by completing quiz questions within eBooks and then exchange these points for rewards.

My Pictures: A child can personalise their avatar and side-panel design

Parent's Help: Handy hints and tips for a parent reading with their child, customised to their child's reading level.

Teacher experience

For you, the teacher, *Bug Club* provides a quick and easy way of allocating reading practice to every child in your class, as well as at-a-glance reports on their attainment. You can log in to your own personalised teacher homepage and access all the planning and assessment tools you need for *Bug Club*.

Book search: You can search by reading level (Book Band, Phonic Phase or Reading Recovery level). Alternatively, you can use *Quick Search* to find books by a keyword search.

Search results: You can see basic eBook information in your results, or choose to see more details about the book.

Open or allocate: From your search results, you can either open eBooks and use these in your planning or teaching in school, or allocate through to children's bookshelves.

Phonics Bug Books and eBooks

Teaching Support

- Flashcards for every Phase
- Fantastic teaching tools
- Lesson plans and assessment support

100% decodable readers with an example eBook for every title

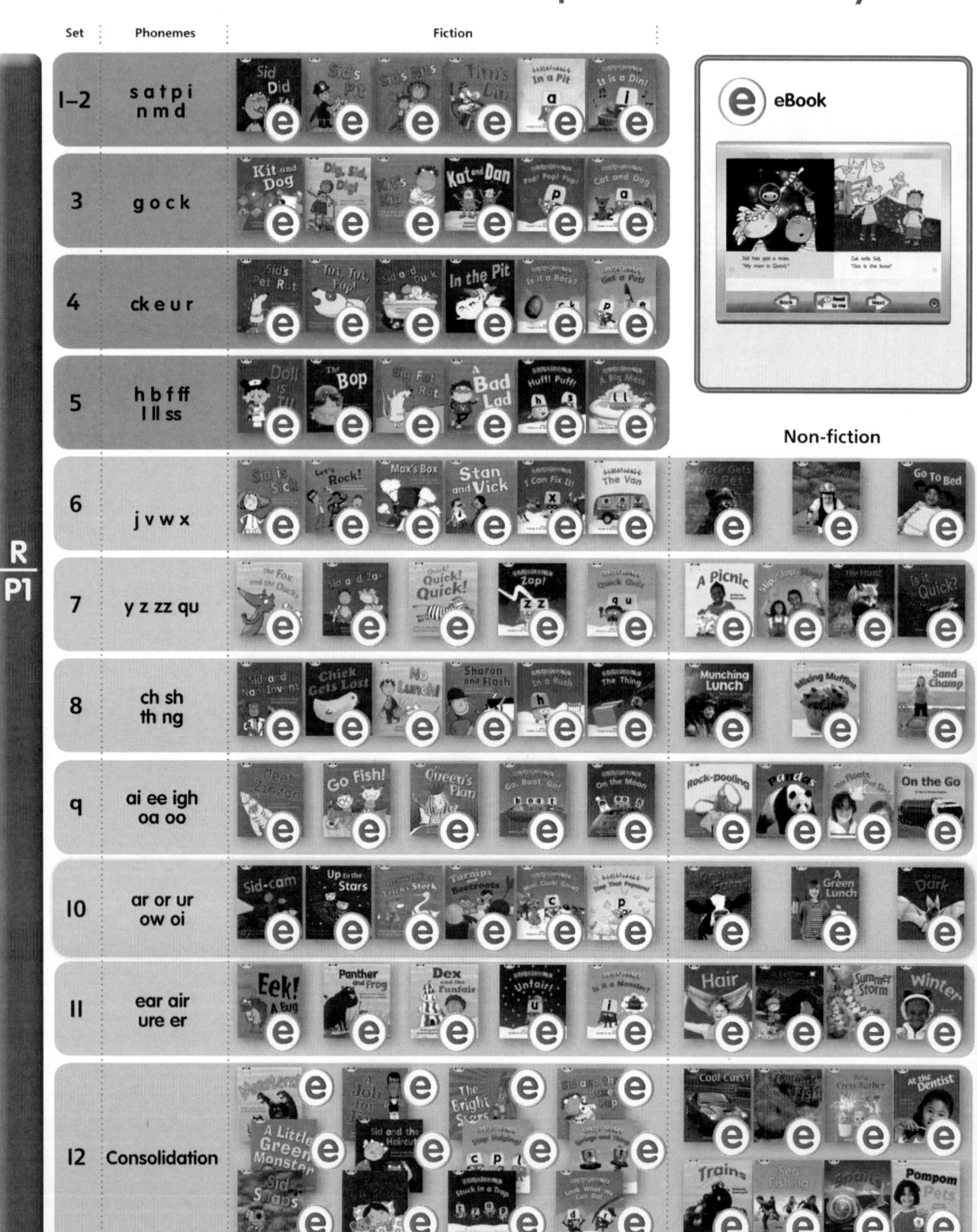

Set	Phonemes	Fiction	Non-fiction
Phase 2			
1–2	s a t p i n m d		
3	g o c k		
4	ck e u r		
5	h b f ff l ll ss		
Phase 3 — R/P1			
6	j v w x		
7	y z zz qu		
8	ch sh th ng		
9	ai ee igh oa oo		
10	ar or ur ow oi		
11	ear air ure er		
Phase 4			
12	Consolidation		

eBook

Some books above were originally published in print form as part of the Rigby Star Phonics series

Phase 5 — 1/P2

Set	Phonemes	Fiction		Non-fiction
13	wh ph	Whizz!		Keeping a Pet
14	ay a–e eigh ey ei (long a)	Runaway Train		Dave's Big Day
15	ea e–e ie ey y (long e)		Easy-Peasy	Sunny Days
16	ie i–e y i (long i)	Butterfly Pie	I Spy	Flying High
17	ow o–e o oe (long o)	The Snow Monster		Animal Skeletons
18	ew ue u–e (long u) u oul (short oo)	Bullfrog is the Best		Cities
19	aw au al our			Creepy-crawly Hunt
20	ir er ear	The Third Whirligig		Sunflowers
21	ou oy			At the Toy Shop
22	eer ere are ear			Meerkats
23	k ck ch	Go-Kart, Go!		
24	ce c sc st se	Kat's Great Act		
25	ge g dge			Different Homes
26	le mb kn gn wr	The Purple Muncher		Dinosaurs
27	tch sh alternatives ea (w)a o	Itch Factor		Rabbits

Bug Club Books and eBooks

Phase	Band	Book Band Level	Fiction	Non-fiction	Comics/Graphic Novels	Phonics Comics
Phase 2	R/P1	Lilac				
Phase 2	R/P1	Pink A — RR1				
Phase 2	R/P1	Pink B — RR2				
Phase 3	R/P1	Red A — RR3				
Phase 3	R/P1	Red B — RR4				
Phase 3	R/P1	Red C — RR5				
Phase 4	1/P2	Yellow A — RR6				
Phase 4	1/P2	Yellow B — RR7				
Phase 4	1/P2	Yellow C — RR8				
Phase 5	1/P2	Blue A — RR9				
Phase 5	1/P2	Blue B — RR10				
Phase 5	1/P2	Blue C — RR11				
Phase 5	1/P2	Green A — RR12				
Phase 5	1/P2	Green B — RR13				
Phase 5	1/P2	Green C — RR14				

Key: 📄 printed book ⓔ eBook ▢ new title, coming Spring 2012

Comes with a Planning and Assessment Guide for each year

Bug Club

	Book Band Level	Fiction	Non-fiction	Comics/Graphic Novels
Phase 5	Orange A **RR15**	Cheese; Dino-soaring; Caspar	Flips in Space; Strawberries at School	
	Orange B **RR16**	Escape; Dino-sitting; Caspar	Goodnight Vacation; Fun Footballs	
	Turquoise A **RR17**	Run; Dino-splashing; Caspar	Cars Cars; Tricking Our Eyes	Surprise!
	Turquoise B **RR18**	Ben 10: Hunted; Just the Job; ...	Can You Do This?; Extreme Living	
Phase 6 (2/P3)	Purple A **RR19**	Ben 10: Tourist Trap; Wrong Jumper; Fire Demon	Mummies; ...	Laugh Out Loud
	Purple B **RR20**	Ben 10: A Small Problem; I Want a Unicorn!; ...	...; Star Wars: Wookiee?	
	Gold A **RR21**	Sports Day; ...	You CAN Try This At...; Fossils	
	Gold B **RR22**	...; Sick As A Parrot; ...	Going into Space; Animals to the Rescue	
Bridging bands between KS1 and KS2	White A	Fright Fort; All At Sea; Dancing Party; **NEW! Poetry**	...; Caring for Exotic Animals	
	White B	Meddlers; Set Sail for Sea; ...; **NEW! Plays**	...; Gross Things	
	Lime A	Meddlers: Tick, Tock Fix the Clock; YUK!; ; **NEW! Poetry**; Moo and the Riddle	Poptropica; Awesome	
	Lime B	Meddlers: Whitley Fields and the Fix; YUK!; ; **NEW! Plays**; Moo and the Riddle	Star Wars: Jedi; About Earth	

23

Assessing progress – Before starting

Before beginning the programme it is useful for children to do some preparatory work on print conventions, letter knowledge and whiteboard use. The following table itemises what the children should have experience of and suggests ways of giving them this experience (competences in italic are optional). For some of the tasks, you will need to use the Magnetic Board feature in the software (you can do this by clicking "Magnetic Board" from the Unit and Session Select Menu).

Competence	Teaching suggestions
Have experience of activities to develop phonological awareness (Phase 1)	To develop children's ability to listen to and identify everyday sounds, play listening games. Provide sequences of sounds for them to remember and to say the location of a particular sound – e.g. the ringing doorbell was the first sound, the barking dog was the second sound etc. Developing listening skills leads to an awareness of phonemes and syllables.
	To focus the children's attention on the structure of words and to develop their familiarity with rhyme and rhythm, provide opportunities to sing songs, nursery rhymes, jingles, raps with music and movement, and skipping games. Collect objects or pictures that rhyme, asking the children to name each object and talk about the rhymes.
	To encourage children to focus on alliteration and initial (onset) sounds, put out objects and pictures and play 'I spy'. Ask the children to think of words beginning with the same sounds – e.g. man, mop, mummy.
	To develop an awareness that language consists of words and sentences, children can play games with spoken sentences of different lengths – e.g. for each sentence, one child comes out to stand at the front for each word. How many children (words) make up the sentence? Can other children generate a new sentence with the same number of words?
	To help children identify rhythm in words (syllables), ask them to use their bodies to act out the syllable beats in a word – e.g. by marching or clapping in time. Progress to asking children to tap the number of syllables in their names and other words, such as Sunday, sunshine, teapot, bathtub, tiptoe.
	To practise oral blending, segment words into phonemes and then say the whole word. For example, say to the children, "Tap your h-ea-d, head."
	To practise oral segmentation, introduce the children to a puppet who can only understand sound-talk. For example, ask the puppet what he or she would like to do. The puppet whispers in the teacher's ear, and the teacher repeats "h-o-p", and then says "hop". Ask the children to see if they can speak in puppet-talk. Get them to say "h-o-p" to the puppet, who responds by hopping up and down.

Assessing progress – Before starting

Competence	Teaching suggestions
Have experience of the conventions of print and the vocabulary of reading, i.e.: • left-to-right directionality • top-to-bottom directionality • words are made up of letters • spaces are used between words • use of lower- and uppercase letters • punctuation • positional words (see right) • illustrations.	Read stories with the children, pointing out and discussing the conventions of print. Use positional words such as *page, top, bottom, start, beginning, end, first, middle, last, right, left.*
Know about alphabetic order (if teaching letter names). *Match lowercase letter names to print.* Be familiar with the interactive screen.	Select the lowercase version of the Magnetic Board and use it to introduce the children to the alphabet. Read the names in order as you point to the letters. Select the Alphabet song button. Play the lowercase version of the Alphabet song with voice accompaniment, and as the children become familiar with it over a few days, encourage them to join in. Tell the children that they are learning the letter names of the alphabet and point out that each letter of the alphabet is being highlighted as it is sung. As they become more secure with the Alphabet song you may wish to switch to the music-only version, by selecting the Lyric tool, and ask a child to point to the letters as they are sung.
Match uppercase letter names to print (if teaching letter names). Know that lower- and uppercase letters correspond to each other.	Repeat the procedures above with the uppercase letters. Discuss with the children the fact that lower- and uppercase letters share the same name. (Later on in the programme, they will find out that they also share the same sound.)
Manipulate items on the screen (if teaching letter names).	Play 'find the letter' games with the children. Say a letter name and ask the children to drag the corresponding letter from the Alphabet panel onto the work area, or to click on the letter to make it appear on the work area. Switch between lower- and uppercase alphabet options when playing this game.
Have sufficient pencil control to make straight lines and circles with adequate firmness and good posture.	Give the children opportunities to use pencil and paper to draw and write.

Assessment

Phonics Bug contains a variety of useful assessment resources to help you ensure that all children are progressing in line with national expectations throughout Reception, Year 1 and Year 2.

The resources help you gauge children's knowledge of the grapheme-phoneme correspondences and their ability to blend (using both real and non-words). These are the skills needed to reach the expected standard for the Phonics Screening Check in Year 1. You can also assess their knowledge of high frequency irregular (tricky) words. The resources can be used at regular intervals to provide an ongoing record of children's attainment. More information about the Phonics Screening Check is available in the *Phonics Bug Prepare and Assess Handbook*, along with a set of reading tests that will help familiarise pupils with the format of the Screening Check.

Ongoing formative assessment

Daily assessment is carried out in two ways. Firstly, through using the Whole-Class Revision section of the Phoneme Sessions you can identify strengths and weaknesses at an early stage and intervene to support those children who need it during the Independent Session.

Additionally, you can monitor how well children complete the independent tasks in order to give an ongoing indicator of how each child is progressing. Feedback about progress should also be given to the children so that they know what they need to do to improve.

Children should also be assessed on their ability to use taught strategies to read unknown words. This should be done individually when they are reading their reading books to you. However, it is important that children should not be asked to guess an unknown word from context or use picture cues.

Self-assessment

Children should be encouraged to practise self-assessment, measured against the learning outcomes for the day. They can also reflect on their own performance through the inclusion of happy and sad faces on the PCMs, which they should tick in accordance with how confident they feel about the task. For further information, see page 15.

Summative assessment

Summative assessment (to be used formatively) is also provided. We suggest you undertake assessment activities regularly throughout the programme. Time can then be allocated to helping children to catch up while they continue in the whole-class programme. It is suggested that you undertake assessment at the end of the *Reception* part of the programme (after Unit 12). This will inform any further teaching and/or consolidation that is deemed necessary.

Assessment and catch-up activities

Letter names and sounds

From the beginning, it will be apparent that some children are slow at learning the letter names and sounds. These children should be kept in the classroom programme, where they will get constant exposure to the role of letters in finding the pronunciation of words. It is helpful for all children to learn the letter formation as each letter sound is learnt – the more multi-sensory information they have about letters, the better they are at consolidating them in memory.

However, spelling work is carried out at the beginning using magnetic letters, so that those slow at learning letter formation are not held back in practising segmenting words for spelling. Children having difficulty in learning letters will be picked up in Assessments 1 and 2.

Blending

Some children will be slow to learn to sound and blend to find out the pronunciation of an unfamiliar word. Again, we recommend that they stay in the classroom programme to get continuous reinforcement of the alphabetic principle, and plenty of exposure to the printed word. This will ensure they do not develop unhelpful approaches to word reading, such as focussing on the letters at the beginning and end of words. Children having difficulty in blending will be picked up in Assessment 5.

Vowel digraphs/trigraphs and phonic rules

Vowel digraphs (covered here in Units 9–11, and more extensively in *Phonics Bug – Key Stage 1*) are difficult for all children. This is where there is the greatest variability in English spelling (e.g. 'ea' has multiple pronunciations, and the long 'e' sound can be spelt in a number of different ways). Inevitably some learning has to be word specific (e.g. 'head' versus 'bead'). It is very useful to also teach certain phonic rules, such as split digraphs (i.e. silent or magic 'e'), although again there are word-specific exceptions that need to be learnt. There are also other useful rules covered in this programme, such as silent letters, and rules for when to double up the final consonant before adding a suffix. Children having difficulty with the digraphs taught in *Phonics Bug – Reception (Primary 1)* will be picked up in Assessments 3 and 4.

Adjacent consonants

Words with adjacent consonants can be read by blending, and do not need to be taught in blocks of words starting, for example, with 'sl' or ending in 'pt'. Our research shows there is much better learning of adjacent consonants by slow learners if they are taught by the synthetic phonics method, so we begin to introduce a few words with adjacent consonants from Unit 6 (start of Phase 3). (If you are following the guidance in *Letters and Sounds* (DfES, 2007), which delays the introduction of adjacent consonants until Phase 4, you may wish to omit these in Units 6–11.) Unit 12 of *Phonics Bug* offers consolidation (or initial) teaching to ensure children understand adjacent consonants in differing positions within words, and longer letter strings (Phase 4 teaching). Children having difficulty with adjacent consonants will be picked up in Assessment 6. You may also wish to use Assessment 6 (adjacent consonants) at the end of Unit 12 to get an impression of how well the children can blend.

Assessment

The chart below outlines areas for assessment, together with suggestions for assessment methods. The necessary resource sheets are provided on pages 29–36.

Phases 2 and 3: Assessments 1, 2, 3, 4 and 5

In Phase 2 (Units 1 to 5), children learn 19 letters of the alphabet and read CVC (consonant-vowel-consonant) words. You can test knowledge of the sounds and names of these letters after Unit 5, but many children will not be able to confidently identify them at this stage. Phase 3 (Units 6–11) covers the remaining 7 letters of the alphabet, and some consonant and vowel digraphs and trigraphs. Testing of the knowledge of the sounds of the letters, digraphs and trigraphs is done individually (Assessments 1 and 3); however, the ability to write them to dictation can be tested in small groups or with the whole class (Assessments 2 and 4). Assessment 5 is used to test blending for reading and segmenting for spelling, and is done individually. Even if children perform poorly on these tests, they should remain in the whole-class teaching programme, as everything is reinforced over and over again in subsequent lessons. It is also good for their self-esteem. Advice on catch-up work can be found on pages 37–38.

Assessment area	Method
Names and sounds of letters	Assessment Sheet 1 is used to test the names and sounds of the alphabet. Point to each lowercase letter in turn, asking the child to tell you the name of the letter and the sound. Repeat with the uppercase letters. You may record the child's response on the sheet.
Writing letters	Assessment Sheet 2 is the score sheet for the writing of the alphabet to dictation. If done at the end of Phase 2, stop after 19 letters on these tests. RESOURCE: ASSESSMENT SHEETS 1 AND 2
Digraphs/ trigraphs	Assessment Sheet 3 tests knowledge of the sounds of the digraphs and trigraphs, and Assessment Sheet 4 is the score sheet for writing them to dictation. The earliest this can be done is at the end of Phase 3 (after Unit 11). RESOURCE: ASSESSMENT SHEETS 3 AND 4
Blending and segmenting CVC words	Carry out individually with children having obvious blending and segmenting problems. 'Nonwords' are used so that children cannot use a partial visual strategy to read them based on words they have seen before. You can tell children that the nonwords are the names of the friends of the animated character in the interactive whiteboard programme. • **Sounding and blending for reading** Show the child the nonwords one at a time, from Assessment Sheet 5, or on flashcards downloaded from the software (see page 14 for instructions on how to access these). Note the accuracy of their decoding on your score sheet, and also whether there are any overt signs of sounding and blending, and if so, how effective it is – e.g. does the child only give the first sound? Does he/she give the right sounds in the wrong order?
Blending and segmenting CVC words (cont'd)	In our experience, a group of children will on average only get around half of these nonwords correct at this stage. However, in the Clackmannanshire study, many of those who got none at all right at this stage were doing well a year later with little or no catch-up work. If you decide to do this test when you have just finished Unit 11, please do bear this in mind. All of the children should continue in the whole-class programme, regardless of how they perform. • **Segmenting for spelling** Read out the nonwords for the child to spell, repeating each nonword until the child has heard it clearly. The child can use his/her magnetic board with the full array of letters; if he/she is writing the letters, have the full alphabet in view. RESOURCE: ASSESSMENT SHEET 5
Reading and spelling not fully decodable common words	Use the words provided as flashcards (downloadable from the software) to assess whether children can read the Phase 3 not fully decodable common words. To assess spelling of these words, pronounce each one for the children to write or spell using their magnetic letters.

Catch-up activities for Phases 2 and 3: Assessments 1, 2, 3, 4 and 5

Assessment area	Method
Names and sound of letters Sounds of digraphs/ trigraphs	Use extra games sessions, selecting the games for the letters, digraphs and trigraphs on which mistakes have been made.
Writing letters	a) Use the relevant letter formation sessions on the interactive whiteboard. b) Go back to the PCMs for each phoneme session.
Blending and segmenting CVC words	Carry out further sounding and blending practice, one-to-one, using the further nonwords provided as flashcards downloaded from the software (see page 14 for instructions on how to access these). It is useful to tape-record each child's attempts, so that pupil and teacher can listen to the attempts together, discussing how accurate they were or what might improve the blending process. Carry out further segmenting and spelling practice, reading out and repeating as necessary the further nonwords from flashcards downloaded from the software. Keep any struggling children in the whole-class programme, and do the catch-up sessions at other times during the day. See pages 37–38 for more advice on how to do this.

Assessment

Phases 4: Assessments 6 and 7

Phase 4 emphasises the reading of nonwords with adjacent consonants. The earliest this assessment can be carried out is after Unit 12.

Assessment area	Method
Blending and segmenting CCVC, CVCC and CCVCC words	Carry out initially for spelling to screen the whole class for difficulties with segmenting. Nonwords are used so that children cannot use a partial visual strategy to read them based on words they have seen before. You can tell the children that the nonwords are the names of friends of the animated character in the interactive whiteboard programme. • **Segmenting for spelling** Read each nonword out clearly, repeating it until the children have heard it properly. A child tested individually can use a magnetic board for spelling. If the children are writing the letters, you can let them see the full alphabet. You might like to note the errors the children make on the assessment sheet provided – e.g. if they only get the first letter right, or write the correct letters in the wrong order. • **Blending for reading** For those children found to have difficulty with the spelling, you might like to test them individually on their reading. When reading nonwords, show the child the nonwords one by one, masking all but the nonword being attempted (if using Assessment Sheet 6). Note on the assessment sheet the errors made. If you tape-record their reading, the child can listen and discuss with you how to improve his/her attempts. You might like to note whether they miss out letters, or just try to read the item as a familiar word. RESOURCE: ASSESSMENT SHEET 6 *The nonwords are also provided on flashcards which can be downloaded from the software (see page 14 for instructions on how to access these).*
Reading and spelling not fully decodable common words	Use the words provided as flashcards (downloadable from the software) to assess that children can read the Phase 4 not fully decodable common words. To assess spelling of these words, pronounce each one for the children to write or spell using their magnetic letters.
Constructing sentences	Ask the children to write a sentence about the picture provided. RESOURCE: ASSESSMENT SHEET 7
Choosing the sentence that makes sense	Ask the children to tick the sentence that makes sense, from the two alternatives given. RESOURCE: ASSESSMENT SHEET 7

Catch-up activities for Assessment Sheet 6

Assessment area	Method
Blending and segmenting CCVC, CVCC and CCVCC words	Carry out further sounding and blending, and segmenting and spelling practice, one-to-one, using the further nonwords provided as flashcards downloaded from the software (see page 14).

Assessment sheet 1

Names and sounds of letters Name: _____

letter	name	sound	letter	name	sound
s			S		
a			A		
t			T		
p			P		
i			I		
n			N		
m			M		
d			D		
g			G		
o			O		
c			C		
k			K		
e			E		
u			U		
r			R		
h			H		
b			B		
f			F		
l			L		
j			J		
v			V		
w			W		
x			X		
y			Y		
z			Z		
q			Q		

Assessment sheet 2

Writing the letters for letter names/letter sounds

Name: _____

1	2	3	4
5	6	7	8
9	10	11	12
13	14	15	16
17	18	19	20
21	22	23	24
25	26		

Assessment sheet 3

Sounds of digraphs and trigraphs   Name: _____

digraphs/trigraphs	sound
ch	
sh	
th	
ng	
ai	
ee	
igh	
oa	
oo (long)	
oo (short)	
ar	
or	
ur	
ow	
oi	
ear	
air	
ure	
er	

Assessment sheet 4

Spelling of digraphs/trigraphs   Name: _____

1	2	3
4	5	6
7	8	9
10	11	12
13	14	15
16	17	
18	19	

Assessment sheet 5

Blending and segmenting Name: _____

Nonword	Blending notes
kig	
dal	
bok	
mep	
san	
bip	
nos	
cuk	
ped	
jul	

Nonword	Segmenting notes
rin	
nop	
weg	
dut	
yab	
lem	
cam	
fon	
zun	
hib	

Assessment sheet 6

Blending and segmenting CCVC and CVCC words

Name: _____ Date: _____

A) CCVC

Nonword	Blending Notes	Nonword	Segmenting Notes
stib		crup	
blat		snig	
brod		skap	
twop		speg	
slaf		plon	
flem		prin	
swip		drog	
gluf		trub	
clum		smat	
frem		gred	

B) CVCC

Nonword	Blending Notes	Nonword	Segmenting Notes
tond		tund	
dist		dest	
fent		fant	
hong		ting	
kump		kemp	
pask		posk	
relt		ralt	
saft		suft	
musp		mosp	
bink		hink	

Assessment sheet 6 continued

Blending and segmenting CCVCC words

Name: _____   Date: _____

C) CCVCC

Nonword	Blending Notes	Nonword	Segmenting Notes
blapt		blamp	
slest		slelt	
crilk		crint	
fromp		spind	
spunt		plusp	
plasp		frast	
stend		stemp	
spimp		crind	
plont		blosp	
crupt		plupt	

Assessment sheet 7

Name: _____

1 Write about the picture.

_____

_____

2 Tick the sentences that make sense.

The cat hid in the tent. ☐
The cat hid in the bent. ☐

The queen had a big sing. ☐
The queen had a big ring. ☐

Gran had sent Josh a rift. ☐
Gran had sent Josh a gift. ☐

Assessment and catch-up work in preparation for Key Stage 1

Catch-up work for learning letter sounds and letter formation

This procedure can be done at any point in the programme, but we have outlined here a scenario for early detection and support for slower learners.

Around 2 months into the programme, Unit 7 has been completed with the whole class, and all 26 letters of the alphabet have been introduced. The teacher has decided to carry out a test of the children's knowledge of the sounds of the letters of the alphabet (Assessment 1), and the writing of those sounds to dictation (Assessment 2).

As she knows from the whole-class sessions that she has a small group of children who only know a few letter sounds, the teacher now has to decide whether to continue to keep these children together with the whole class or to form ability groups. As previously taught letter sounds are reinforced on a daily basis with the whole class, the teacher thinks that if she forms, within the classroom, a nurture/needs group for the three or four slower learning children to target their specific learning needs, they may be able to keep up with their class mates, which will boost their self-esteem and give them a feeling of social inclusion. Four is generally considered to be the optimum size for such a nurture/needs group, to allow for individual efforts and co-operative learning.

Although the teacher knows that, ultimately, these children may need 1:1 individually tailored support programmes, Assessments 1 and 2 indicate that the 4 children are all needing to do extra work on the letter d. That is, they are not sure of the letter sound and are having difficulty in forming the letter. She also feels that it would be useful for them to consolidate their learning of all the letter sounds in Unit 2.

Revisiting the sound for 'd'

The teacher can set aside an area in the classroom for the group of four children with a table and four chairs. They will need:

- facilities for operating the programme on the interactive whiteboard or a laptop computer
- access to materials which will be needed, e.g. magnetic boards, magnetic letters, individual pupil whiteboards, black marker pens, a tray of damp sand, soft modelling clay
- a fresh PCM for /d/ for each pupil.

At the start of the session, to let the children know their learning target, the teacher selects the Sounds tab for the children to see the "This is 'd'" video clip from Unit 2 (Phase 2). She then asks a child to find the letter 'd' and to pull it up onto the whiteboard or computer screen. She then clicks on the audio tool and clicks on 'd' to hear its sound. All of the children repeat the sound. Each child is then invited to select 'd', click on it to hear its sound and to say it at the same time. The teacher clicks on 'd' again and all of the children say the sound. How well did the children do?

Revisiting visual recognition of d

While still in the Sounds tab, the teacher clicks on the Asset bank, and each child gets a chance to circle the letter d in a word ('stand', 'damp', 'add' and 'Adam'), saying whether it is in the middle, the beginning or the end of the word. They do not read the words. Now the teacher can select the Follow-up tab and asset bank words. Another set of words will appear for the children to circle the letter 'd' in each word again, saying whether it is in the middle, the beginning or the end of the word. Finally, children are asked to complete this task on their PCM sheet, circling the letter d in each word. How well did the children do?

Revisiting writing d

The teacher then clicks on the Writing tab, and clicks on Show to get a demonstration of how to write the letter 'd'. The children form the letter in the damp sand using their index finger and saying the sound for d. Then the teacher clicks on Show again, and, using their own whiteboards and black marker pens, the children follow the instructions for forming the letter, saying the letter sound as they finish it. They can look at the whiteboard or computer screen to see how well they have done. The children can then use the Unit 2 PCM sheet for d again, where they will practise forming the letter d. Some children may benefit from work forming the letter using modelling clay.

Games to reinforce d, and all the letters sounds in Unit 2

The Unit 2 games (including all of the letter sounds taught by the end of Unit 2) were first introduced to the class through the daily Lesson Plans for Unit 3. These games will be motivating for the four children, but will also enable the teacher to observe and evaluate the success or otherwise of each pupil's contribution to each game played. Selecting the Sounds category for Games, each child in turn can have a go at identifying the letters from the sounds. Then they can use the Reading category to see these letter sounds in the context of words, and use the Spelling category to reinforce selecting letters to match the sounds they hear.

Reassess learning of Unit 2 Sounds

The next day, the teacher lays out on a magnetic board for each child, the letters: s a t p i n m d. She asks each child to give the sound for each letter as she points to it. Then she re-arranges the letters and says each letter sound, asking them to point to the letter. Children still having difficulty can repeat the procedure above and spend more time playing the Unit 2 Games.

Assessment and catch-up work in preparation for Key Stage 1

Catch-up work for children having problems with blending and segmenting

Support work for blending for reading

Children who are slow to learn letter sounds may also have problems with blending (but not necessarily so). Other children may learn letter sounds with ease but nevertheless have difficulty in blending. What is important in the synthetic phonics approach is that children learn to track sequentially through words from left to right using letter-sound information, in order to read unfamiliar words. We recommend a smooth co-articulation of the sounds in words, spending as little time as possible pronouncing the letter sounds individually.

When children are faced with real words for blending practice, they may have seen them before and so try to recognise them on the basis of partial visual cues. This visual approach may slow down the acquisition of an extensive sight vocabulary, as many words look similar. The synthetic phonics method is designed to develop a form of sight word reading that is underpinned by all-through-the-word letter-sound information. Although slower learners often have short-term memory problems, we have found that sounding and blending practice actually increases their memory spans.

For children having difficulty with blending, we recommend carrying out some support work with *nonwords*; this means that they cannot guess what the item is, so the child has to blend the letter sounds together in order to pronounce it. You can tell the children that these are the names of children in a fictional book!

Assessment

For the assessment, you can use the nonwords on the *Phonics Bug Flashcards*. There are flashcards for the simple CVC nonwords used on Assessment Sheet 5 and Assessment Sheet 6 (which contains adjacent consonants). For Key Stage 1, there are nonwords for Phase 5 and Phase 6 assessments after Units 27 and 30. The flashcards can also be printed off from the software (see 'Print Material' on page 14).

In this scenario, the class has been tested on Assessment Sheet 1, and the children know the letter sounds. They are then tested on Assessment Sheet 5. A small group of children have difficulty in reading these nonwords; it is useful to write on the assessment sheet the mistakes that they make, e.g. do they miss out letters or try to read the items as familiar words?

Catch-up

For support work, new nonwords can be found on the Catch-up: Nonwords flashcards. These occur after Unit 11 and Unit 12, and contain CVC nonwords, and nonwords with adjacent consonants.

Using these nonword cards, the child works through each nonword, blending the letters sounds from left to right. Our research shows that practising this approach is very effective in developing reading skills even in 12 year old secondary pupils.

It may be helpful to use plastic letters on a magnetic board while doing this, so that the letters can be pushed together from left to right as they blend. A game can be made by putting the magnetic letters into two piles, vowels and consonants, and getting the child to select two consonants and a vowel, and blending the letters together (which might produce some real words).

It would also be useful to make sure that the child applies their blending skills when reading text. Your session might include work with an appropriate *Phonics Bug* decodable reader; when the child hesitates over a word, they should be encouraged to sound and blend it.

Support work for segmenting for spelling

Segmenting for spelling involves children having awareness of phonemes in spoken words. However, research has shown that phonemic awareness skills are best developed through learning to read and spell.

First of all, make sure that the child can write or select magnetic letters for all of the letter sounds on Assessment Sheet 2. The children then carry out the segmentation test on Assessment Sheet 5. Read out each nonword clearly, repeating it until the child has heard it properly and can repeat it correctly. Ask the child to write down or select a magnetic letter for the first sound they hear. Then they should say the item again and pick out the next sound and write or select the appropriate letter. Continue like this until the whole item has been attempted, noting down the problems they experience. They may have problems like not repeating the item accurately, not keeping their place, or finding the vowel hard to identify.

The nonwords for segmentation practice are also available on flashcards. Work through these, helping the child segment the words into phonemes in sequential order; using nonwords will help them concentrate on the constituent phonemes. As each word is segmented into phonemes, they should attempt to write the grapheme or select the appropriate magnetic letter. They can then sound and blend the letters to check their spelling.

Can all of the children be kept together for phonics teaching?

In our study in Clackmannanshire we found that the children could be kept together for the first and second year of schooling for phonics work. Although ability groups were not formed, there were very low levels of underachievement. For example, at the end of the second year at school only 2.2% (i.e. 6 out of 268) children had reading ages more than a year below their chronological age, and none were so far behind in spelling, despite around half of the children coming from areas of deprivation. This means that there were no groups of children performing at a Phase 2 level in (the equivalent of) Year 1 classes.

What's next?

Units 1 to 12 in *Phonics Bug* - Reception (Primary 1) take children through to the end of Phase 4, the recommended teaching for a child's first year at school. There are 18 further Units in *Phonics Bug* (Units 13-30), which will take children through to the end of Key Stage 1 (Primary 3). Using your professional judgement, you may decide your class is ready to make a start on *Phonics Bug – Key Stage 1 (Primary 2 and 3)* in the first year of school. *Phonics Bug* is an incremental programme, and so the pace at which you move through the Units can be set by your class.

Units 13–30 introduce children to alternative ways of pronouncing and spelling the graphemes they have already been taught, as well as introducing new graphemes for reading. For instance, they develop the concept that some vowel sounds can be represented in more than one way (e.g. 'ai', 'ay' and 'a-e' for the long 'a' sound) and that sometimes the same grapheme is used to represent different sounds (e.g. 'ea' as in 'bead' and 'head'). Common silent-letter digraphs are introduced as well as the concept of root words, prefixes and suffixes. Throughout these Units children learn how to tackle reading and spelling polysyllabic words by applying phonic rules.

The following table presents an overview of *Phonics Bug* Units 13 to 30.

Phase	Unit	Focus	Not fully decodeable (Irregular words)/ High-frequency words
5	13	zh wh ph	oh their
	14	ay a–e eigh/ey/ei (long a)	Mr Mrs
	15	ea e-e ie/ey/y (long e)	looked called asked
	16	ie i-e y i (long i)	water where
	17	ow o-e o/oe (long o)	who again
	18	ew ue u-e (long u) u/oul (short u)	thought through
	19	aw au al	work laughed because
	20	ir er ear	Thursday Saturday thirteen thirty
	21	ou oy	different any many
	22	ere/eer are/ear	eyes friends
	23	c k ck ch	two once
	24	ce/ci/cy sc/stl se	great clothes
	25	ge/gi/gy dge	it's I'm I'll I've
	26	le mb kn/gn wr	don't can't didn't
	27	tch sh ea (w)a o	first second third
6	28	Suffix endings: -ing, -ed (morphemes)	clearing gleaming rained mailed
	29	Suffix plurals: -s, -es (plural morphemes)	man/men mouse /mice foot/feet tooth/teeth sheep/sheep
	30	Prefix morphemes: re-, un- Prefix + root + suffix	vowel consonant prefix suffix syllable

Guide to teaching Sessions

Every Phoneme Session in the programme follows exactly the same pattern of teaching (with the exception of Unit 1), as does every Language Session. There is a Language Session for each unit (group of letters). The pattern and delivery method of teaching each Session is described here. You are advised to use these pages to familiarise yourself with the method of teaching before you begin the programme. Pages 43-106 give you a detailed plan describing the content of each Session. There is also a 'Guide' button on the software, which will act as an *aide-memoire*.

Limited interactive whiteboard access

If you have only limited access to an interactive whiteboard, you can:

- Use the resource cards and writing on the board to substitute for the Reading Teaching Elements, the asset bank contents and free-writing on screen.
- Use magnetic letters for all uses of the electronic Magnetic letters.
- Carry out your own demonstrations of letter formation, letter-sound articulation and blending.

Generic lesson guidance

Remember that each Phoneme and Language Session should feature the following:

- The Alphabet song to begin and end every Session (if letter names are taught)
- Learning intentions and desired outcomes discussed at the beginning of each lesson
- Learning outcomes discussed at the end of each lesson
- The necessary next steps (online pupil games, relevant Unit PCMs for guided independent work, and relevant reading books)

The daily lesson plans

Each Phoneme Session is divided into Revision and Lesson (with the exception of Unit 1, Sessions 1-4). The Revision Session ensures that the children have retained all the teaching from their previous Sessions – grapheme-phoneme correspondences; blending for reading and segmenting for spelling of the relevant words. It is advisable to read the Lesson part of the session before the Revision part of the session as this will give you a better understanding of how to build up phoneme knowledge. Each Language session is divided into Irregular (key words) and Lesson. Remember that the programme is effective if the children are active participants in the lessons.

Alphabet song

The Alphabet Song, automatically highlighting the letters, can begin and end every Session. It helps children to learn the alphabet and to practise letter-name correspondence. One version of the song includes accompaniment and singing, but before long the children can sing the song on their own, so the second version of the song needs only the accompaniment with one child coming out to point to the letters as they are sung. The software provides for singing in both lower case and upper case letters.

Glossary of terms

Adjacent consonants two or more letters that represent two or more phonemes, e.g. 'fr' beginning the word "fridge"

Blend drawing together the constituent phonemes of a written word in order to read it

Digraph two successive letters that represent one phoneme, e.g. 'oa', 'ck', etc.

Grapheme letter or combination of letters that represent a phoneme, e.g. 'r', 'ch'

Phoneme the smallest unit of sound that changes a word's meaning; it can be represented by one or several letters, e.g. /a/ or /sh/

Segment breaking down the sounds of a spoken word into phonemes in order to spell it

Trigraph three successive letters representing one phoneme, e.g. 'igh'

Guide to teaching Sessions

Unit 4

Target phoneme /r/ written as 'r'

The target phonemes are stated at the start of each session

INTRODUCTION
- Play the alphabet song twice, once with voice accompaniment, children listening and singing along with accompaniment, and once with children singing along to the music without voice accompaniment.
- Discuss with the children the learning intentions for the day.

REVISION
[previously taught grapheme–phoneme correspondences; blending phonemes for reading; segmenting spoken words for spelling]
- Go through the Revision screens at a brisk pace.
- Watch out for any children who have not remembered the phonemes or the graphemes.

LESSON

Sounds
- Choose the relevant lesson session.
- Play the "This is 'r'" video once through.
- Say the phoneme /r/, and ask the children to repeat it after you. Make sure you keep the sound pure and encourage the children to do the same.

Visual Search
- Bring up the words from the asset bank onto the Work area. Ask the children to highlight the 'r' in each of the words, saying whether r's position is at the beginning, the middle or the end of the word. Do not pronounce the words.

Reading
- Click the Reading tab for children to see the printed word. Note: Children *are not told* the word. The word is broken down into its constituent phonemes. Ask children to say each of the phonemes in the word.
- Click Blend to watch and hear the Bug's demonstration of how to blend the word.
- Click Undo and then ask a child to come to the Work area and move the arrow along. Encourage the whole class to blend the sounds out loud as the arrow moves along pushing the letters together. We recommend a smooth articulation of the sounds for blending.
- Work through each of the words in sequence. Click ▶ to change words.

Spelling
- The children return to their seats.
- Start by selecting the Words tab. Remember, the children do not see the word. Click Say to hear the word and ask the children to repeat it. Then ask the children to use their magnetic letters to make the word on their own magnetic boards, saying the word every time they look for a letter. Follow the procedure for word spelling on page 47.
- Ask a child to come up to the Work area to make the word. Did everyone get it right?
- Ask a child to use the arrow to push the letters together. Encourage the class to blend the word out loud.
- Repeat for the remaining word under the Words tab.
- Under the Pictures tab, click Show to display the image. You and the children say the picture word and proceed to spell it as before. Repeat if there is more than one image.
- Select the Spelling video and play it once through.

Writing
- Ask the children to find the 'r' letter among their magnetic letters and to feel the shape of it. Click Show and ask the children to look and listen as the lowercase letter is formed.
- "Skywrite" the letter in the air, and ask the children to do the same as you say how to form the letter.
- Ask children to tell you how to write the letter as you write it on the empty Work area.
- Ask children to try to write the letter themselves using paper and pencil or individual whiteboard and pen.
- Select uppercase and repeat when you think this to be appropriate for your children.

WRAP-UP
- Recap the learning intentions with the children.
- Play the "This is 'r'" video again, then play the alphabet song and encourage the children to sing along, signifying the end of the session.

Learning intentions are to:
- recap what we know
- say the /r/ phoneme
- find the letter 'r'
- read words with 'r' in
- spell words with 'r' in
- write the letter 'r'

Focus content: revision

Letters and Sounds
d, g, o, c, k, ck, e, u
Reading
sum, mud, cup, sun
Writing and Spelling
k, ck, e, u
us, cut, mug, suck

This panel gives you at-a-glance information about the content of the session

Focus content: lesson

Sounds
"This is 'r'" video
Visual search
trip, rat, rap, print
Reading
Audio: run, rag, rut, rim
No audio: rap, rug, rid, rock
Spelling
Words tab: ran, red
Pictures tab: rat, rod
Video: rip, red
Writing
r

Next steps
- Play the online pupil games for Unit 3
- Complete the PCM for Unit 4 (r)
- Read Phonics Bug books that practise g, o, c, k:
  Cat and Dog
  Dig, Sid, Dig!
  Kat and Dan
  Kit and Dog
  Kit's Kip
  Pop! Pop! Pop!

Suggested next steps in the form of guided independent work and Phonics Bug reading books are given throughout

61

Guide to teaching Sessions

Language sessions enable children to apply the skills taught in prior sessions to read and spell irregular words, captions and sentences

Notes to the teacher explain any particular points or exceptions

Unit 4

Language session

After: ck, e, u, r

INTRODUCTION
- Play the alphabet song twice, once with voice accompaniment, children listening and singing along with accompaniment, and once with children singing along to the music without voice accompaniment.
- Discuss with the children the learning intentions for the day.

IRREGULAR

Reading
- Click Show to display the words, and ask/teach the children how to read them. Click Answer to hear the correct pronunciation. Ask the children to repeat it.
- Explain that 'e' and 'u' are vowels like 'a', 'i', and 'o'.
- If 'the' is being used before a word beginning with a consonant, the 'e' sounds a short /e/; if it is being used before a word beginning with a vowel, the 'e' sounds /ee/. Depending on the geographical region you are in, the 'e' can also sound /i/.
- In the words 'no' and 'go', 'o' sounds like its letter name, pronounced /oa/.

Spelling
- Click Say to hear the word, and ask the children to repeat it.
- Put the word into a sentence, so that the children understand its meaning, for example, "Close the door", "There were no sweets left", "Let's go to the park".
- Ask children to say the word, help to select the lowercase magnetic letters and drag each letter into its empty box.
- Ask the children to read the word.
- Repeat for the remaining words.

LESSON

Reading
- Click Show to display the caption, and ask the children to read it.
- Click Answer to see whether they are right.
- Repeat for the sentence. Remind the children that a sentence starts with a capital letter and ends with a full stop.

Spelling
- Click Say to hear the caption and ask the children to repeat it.
- Ask the children to help you to select the lowercase magnetic letters and drag the letters to the empty boxes on the Work area.
- Ask the children to read the caption.
- Repeat the procedure for the remaining captions.

Writing
- The children return to their seats.
- Click Say to hear the caption and ask the children to repeat it.
- Ask the children to tell you how to write the caption on the lines provided.
- Clear the screen. Ask the children to say the caption and try to write it using paper and pencil or individual whiteboard and pen.
- Click Answer to check whether they are right.
- Repeat for the remaining captions.

Follow-up
- Display the picture. You and the children say the caption for the picture (a red pen).
- Ask the children to spell the caption, using pencil and paper.
- Click on the picture itself to show the caption and ask the children to read it.

WRAP-UP
- Recap the learning intentions with the children.
- Play the alphabet song again and encourage the children to sing along, signifying the end of the session.

Learning intentions are to:
- learn to read and spell irregular words "the", "no" and "go"
- learn to read and spell short captions

Focus content: irregular

Reading
the, no, go
Spelling
the, no, go

Focus content: lesson

Reading
no pets in the den
Mick and Ken go to get nuts.
Spelling
a mug, ten men, run in the sun
Writing
a mug, ten men, run in the sun
Follow-up
Picture shows: a red pen

Next steps
- Play the online language pupil games for Unit 4
- Complete the language PCM for Unit 4
- Read Phonics Bug books that practise ck, e, u, r:
    Get a Pet!
    In the Pit
    Is it a Rock?
    Sid and Duck
    Sid's Pet Rat
    Tut, Tut, Pup!

Learning intentions are provided for each session

62

Target phoneme /s/ written as 's'

INTRODUCTION
- Play the alphabet song twice, once with voice accompaniment, children listening and singing along with accompaniment, and once with children singing along to the music without voice accompaniment.
- Discuss with the children the learning intentions for the day.

LESSON
Sounds
- Choose the relevant lesson session.
- Play the "This is 's'" video once through.
- Say the phoneme /s/, and ask the children to repeat it after you. Make sure you keep the sound pure and encourage the children to do the same.

Visual Search
- Bring up the words from the asset bank onto the Work area. Ask the children to highlight the 's' in each of the words, saying whether s's position is at the beginning, the middle or the end of the word. Do not pronounce the words.
- If appropriate, point out that 's' sometimes has a /z/ sound, often at the end of words, as in "is" and "has".

Writing
- The children return to their seats.
- Ask the children to find the 's' letter among their magnetic letters and to feel the shape of it. Click Show and ask the children to look and listen as the lowercase letter is formed.
- "Skywrite" the letter in the air, and ask the children to do the same as you say how to form the letter.
- Ask children to tell you how to write the letter as you write it on the empty Work area.
- Ask children to try to write the letter themselves using paper and pencil or individual whiteboard and pen.
- Select uppercase and repeat when you think this to be appropriate for your children.

WRAP-UP
- Recap the learning intentions with the children.
- Play the "This is 's'" video again, then play the alphabet song and encourage the children to sing along, signifying the end of the session.

Learning intentions are to:
- say the /s/ phoneme
- find the letter 's'
- write the letter 's'

Focus content: lesson

Sounds
"This is 's'" video
Visual search
pants, Stan, past, spins
Writing
s

Next steps
- Complete the PCM for Unit 1 (s)

Unit 1

Unit 1

Target phoneme /a/ written as 'a'

INTRODUCTION
- Play the alphabet song twice, once with voice accompaniment, children listening and singing along with accompaniment, and once with children singing along to the music without voice accompaniment.
- Discuss with the children the learning intentions for the day.

LESSON

Sounds
- Choose the relevant lesson session.
- Play the "This is 'a'" video once through.
- Say the phoneme /a/, and ask the children to repeat it after you. Make sure you keep the sound pure and encourage the children to do the same.

Visual Search
- Bring up the words from the asset bank onto the Work area. Ask the children to highlight the 'a' in each of the words, saying whether a's position is at the beginning, the middle or the end of the word. Do not pronounce the words.
- If appropriate, explain the regional variation in the way the 'a' sound in words such as "ask" and "past" is pronounced.
- Explain that all words are made up of consonants and vowels.
- Explain that 'a' is a vowel.
- Ensure that the children are aware that 'a' is a letter, but it is also a word, e.g. "a tap".
- Write "a tap" on the whiteboard. Point out the space between "a" and "tap" and explain that there is always a space between the two words.
- Explain to the children the difference between a word, e.g. "tap", and a caption, e.g. "a tap".

Writing
- The children return to their seats.
- Ask the children to find the 'a' letter among their magnetic letters and to feel the shape of it. Click Show and ask the children to look and listen as the lowercase letter is formed.
- "Skywrite" the letter in the air, and ask the children to do the same as you say how to form the letter.
- Ask children to tell you how to write the letter as you write it on the empty Work area.
- Ask children to try to write the letter themselves using paper and pencil or individual whiteboard and pen.
- Select uppercase and repeat when you think this to be appropriate for your children.

WRAP-UP
- Recap the learning intentions with the children.
- Play the "This is 'a'" video again, then play the alphabet song and encourage the children to sing along, signifying the end of the session.

Learning intentions are to:
- say the /a/ phoneme
- find the letter 'a'
- write the letter 'a'

Focus content: lesson

Sounds
"This is 'a'" video
Visual search
act, zebra, sat, Amanda
Writing
a

Next steps
- Complete the PCM for Unit 1 (a)

Target phoneme /t/ written as 't'

INTRODUCTION
- Play the alphabet song twice, once with voice accompaniment, children listening and singing along with accompaniment, and once with children singing along to the music without voice accompaniment.
- Discuss with the children the learning intentions for the day.

LESSON

Sounds
- Choose the relevant lesson session.
- Play the "This is 't'" video once through.
- Say the phoneme /t/, and ask the children to repeat it after you. Make sure you keep the sound pure and encourage the children to do the same.

Visual Search
- Bring up the words from the asset bank onto the Work area. Ask the children to highlight the 't' in each of the words, saying whether t's position is at the beginning, the middle or the end of the word. Do not pronounce the words.

Writing
- The children return to their seats.
- Ask the children to find the 't' letter among their magnetic letters and to feel the shape of it. Click Show and ask the children to look and listen as the lowercase letter is formed.
- "Skywrite" the letter in the air, and ask the children to do the same as you say how to form the letter.
- Ask children to tell you how to write the letter as you write it on the empty Work area.
- Ask children to try to write the letter themselves using paper and pencil or individual whiteboard and pen.
- Select uppercase and repeat when you think this to be appropriate for your children.

WRAP-UP
- Recap the learning intentions with the children.
- Play the "This is 't'" video again, then play the alphabet song and encourage the children to sing along, signifying the end of the session.

Unit 1

Learning intentions are to:
- say the phoneme /t/
- find the letter 't'
- write the letter 't'

Focus content: lesson

Sound
"This is 't'" video
Visual search
at, tin, tent, Scott
Writing
t

Next steps
- Complete the PCM for Unit 1 (t)

Unit 1

Target phoneme /p/ written as 'p'

INTRODUCTION
- Play the alphabet song twice, once with voice accompaniment, children listening and singing along with accompaniment, and once with children singing along to the music without voice accompaniment.
- Discuss with the children the learning intentions for the day.

LESSON

Sounds
- Choose the relevant lesson session.
- Play the "This is 'p'" video once through.
- Say the phoneme /p/, and ask the children to repeat it after you. Make sure you keep the sound pure and encourage the children to do the same.

Visual Search
- Bring up the words from the asset bank onto the Work area. Ask the children to highlight the 'p' in each of the words, saying whether p's position is at the beginning, the middle or the end of the word. Do not pronounce the words.

Writing
- The children return to their seats.
- Ask the children to find the 'p' letter among their magnetic letters and to feel the shape of it. Click Show and ask the children to look and listen as the lowercase letter is formed.
- "Skywrite" the letter in the air, and ask the children to do the same as you say how to form the letter.
- Ask children to tell you how to write the letter as you write it on the empty Work area.
- Ask children to try to write the letter themselves using paper and pencil or individual whiteboard and pen.
- Select uppercase and repeat when you think this to be appropriate for your children.

WRAP-UP
- Recap the learning intentions with the children.
- Play the "This is 'p'" video again, then play the alphabet song and encourage the children to sing along, signifying the end of the session.

Learning intentions are to:
- say the /p/ phoneme
- find the letter 'p'
- write the letter 'p'

Focus content: lesson

Sound
"This is 'p'" video
Visual search
stop, Penny, pat, puppet
Writing
p

Next steps
- Complete the PCM for Unit 1 (p)

Description of the Blending Process
Before embarking on the Reading and Spelling elements of the Sessions that follow, you may find this description of the blending process helpful.
- Children see the word but are *not told* what it is – e.g. 'sip' (see online version of Unit 2 'i' Lesson, under the Reading tab).
- They sound out each separate phoneme in the word: /s/ /i/ /p/.
- They repeat each phoneme slowly and smoothly, stretching each sound out into its adjoining sound without a pause and giving the same emphasis to each sound, blending the sounds together to achieve the single sound of the complete word. This is known as 'co-articulation'. In the online version, one child physically carries out the blending process of the letters by pushing along the green arrow, while the rest of the children blend the sounds together to read the word. We recommend a smooth co-articulation of sounds for blending.
- Children read the word as one complete sound.

Unit 1

Target phonemes /s/, /a/, /t/, /p/ written as 's', 'a', 't', 'p'

INTRODUCTION
- Play the alphabet song twice, once with voice accompaniment, children listening and singing along with accompaniment, and once with children singing along to the music without voice accompaniment.
- Discuss with the children the learning intentions for the day.

REVISION
- Go through the Revision screens at a brisk pace.
- Watch out for any children who have not remembered the phonemes or the graphemes.

LESSON

Reading
- Click the Reading tab to see a printed word (e.g. tap). Note: Children *are not told* the word. The word is broken down into its constituent phonemes (i.e. /t/ /a/ /p/). Ask children to say each of the phonemes in the word.
- Click Blend to watch and hear the Bug's demonstration of how to blend the word.
- Click Undo and then ask a child to come to the Work area and move the arrow along. Encourage the whole class to blend the sounds out loud as the arrow moves along pushing the letters together. We recommend a smooth articulation of the sounds for blending.
- Work through each of the words in sequence.

Spelling
- The children return to their seats.
- Spell words using the four phonemes. Start by selecting the Words tab. Click Say to hear the word. Ask children to repeat it. Note: Children *do not* see the word.
- Ask children to say the word (e.g. pats) and the first phoneme (i.e. /p/).
- You and a child select the appropriate lowercase letter and drag it up to the first space provided in the Work area.
- Ask children to say the word again and the second phoneme (i.e. /a/).
- As before, select and drag up the appropriate letter to the next (second) space provided in the Work area.
- Repeat the procedure for the third and fourth phonemes, dragging up the appropriate letters to the third and fourth spaces provided in the Work area.
- Ask the child to push the letters together by clicking on the green arrow and moving it along while the whole class blends the sounds out loud.
- Select the next word and click Say for children to hear the word (e.g. taps). Ask children to use their magnetic letters to make the word on their own magnetic boards. Remind them to say the word and the appropriate phoneme before they select and place each letter on their board.
- Ask a child to come up to the Work area to make the word. Did everyone get it right? Select the Pictures tab. Click Show to display the image and ask children to say with you the appropriate word for the picture and proceed to spell it as before using their magnetic boards. Repeat if there is more than one image.

WRAP-UP
- Recap the learning intentions with the children.
- Play the video clip for one of the phonemes again, then play the alphabet song and encourage the children to sing along, signifying the end of the session.

Learning intentions are to:
- recap what we know
- say the phonemes /s/, /a/, /t/ and /p/
- read words with 's', 'a', 't' and 'p' in them
- spell words with 's', 'a', 't' and 'p' in them
- write the letters 's', 'a', 't' and 'p'

Focus content: revision

Letters and Sounds
s, a, t, p

Writing and Spelling
s, a, t, p

Focus content: lesson

Reading
Audio: tap, pat, sat, as
No audio: at, sap

Spelling
Words tab: pats, taps
Pictures tab: tap

Unit 2

Target phoneme /i/ written as 'i'

INTRODUCTION
- Play the alphabet song twice, once with voice accompaniment, children listening and singing along with accompaniment, and once with children singing along to the music without voice accompaniment.
- Discuss with the children the learning intentions for the day.

REVISION
[previously taught grapheme–phoneme correspondences; blending phonemes for reading; segmenting spoken words for spelling]
- Go through the Revision screens at a brisk pace.
- Watch out for any children who have not remembered the phonemes or the graphemes.

LESSON

Sounds
- Choose the relevant lesson session.
- Play the "This is 'i'" video once through.
- Say the phoneme /i/, and ask the children to repeat it after you. Make sure you keep the sound pure and encourage the children to do the same.

Visual Search
- Bring up the words from the asset bank onto the Work area. Ask the children to highlight the 'i' in each of the words, saying whether i's position is at the beginning, the middle or the end of the word. Do not pronounce the words.

Reading
- Click the Reading tab for children to see the printed word. Note: Children *are not told* the word. The word is broken down into its constituent phonemes. Ask children to say each of the phonemes in the word.
- Click Blend to watch and hear the Bug's demonstration of how to blend the word.
- Click Undo and then ask a child to come to the Work area and move the arrow along. Encourage the whole class to blend the sounds out loud as the arrow moves along pushing the letters together. We recommend a smooth articulation of the sounds for blending.
- Work through each of the words in sequence. Click ▶ to change words.

Spelling
- The children return to their seats.
- Start by selecting the Words tab. Remember, the children do not see the word. Click Say to hear the word and ask the children to repeat it. Then ask the children to use their magnetic letters to make the word on their own magnetic boards, saying the word every time they look for a letter. Follow the procedure for word spelling on page 47.
- Ask a child to come up to the Work area to make the word. Did everyone get it right?
- Ask a child to use the arrow to push the letters together. Encourage the class to blend the word out loud.
- Repeat for the remaining word under the Words tab.
- Under the Pictures tab, click Show to display the image. You and the children say the picture word and proceed to spell it as before. Repeat if there is more than one image.

Writing
- Ask the children to find the 'i' letter among their magnetic letters and to feel the shape of it. Click Show and ask the children to look and listen as the lowercase letter is formed.
- "Skywrite" the letter in the air, and ask the children to do the same as you say how to form the letter.
- Ask children to tell you how to write the letter as you write it on the empty Work area.
- Ask children to try to write the letter themselves using paper and pencil or individual whiteboard and pen.
- Select uppercase and repeat when you think this to be appropriate for your children.

WRAP-UP
- Recap the learning intentions with the children.
- Play the "This is 'i'" video again, then play the alphabet song and encourage the children to sing along, signifying the end of the session.

Learning intentions are to:
- recap what we know
- say the /i/ phoneme
- find the letter 'i'
- read words with 'i' in
- spell words with 'i' in
- write the letter 'i'

Focus content: revision

Letters and Sounds
s, a, t, p
Reading
as, tap, pat, sat
Writing and Spelling
s, a, t, p
at, sap

Focus content: lesson

Sounds
"This is 'i'" video
Visual search
in, it, pin, tin
Reading
Audio: it, pip, pit, sip
No audio: tip, pips
Spelling
Words tab: is, sips
Pictures tab: sit
Writing
i

Next steps
- Complete the PCM for Unit 2 (i)

Unit 2

Target phoneme /n/ written as 'n'

INTRODUCTION
- Play the alphabet song twice, once with voice accompaniment, children listening and singing along with accompaniment, and once with children singing along to the music without voice accompaniment.
- Discuss with the children the learning intentions for the day.

REVISION
[previously taught grapheme–phoneme correspondences; blending phonemes for reading; segmenting spoken words for spelling]
- Go through the Revision screens at a brisk pace.
- Watch out for any children who have not remembered the phonemes or the graphemes.

LESSON

Sounds
- Choose the relevant lesson session.
- Play the "This is 'n'" video once through.
- Say the phoneme /n/, and ask the children to repeat it after you. Make sure you keep the sound pure and encourage the children to do the same.

Visual Search
- Bring up the words from the asset bank onto the Work area. Ask the children to highlight the 'n' in each of the words, saying whether n's position is at the beginning, the middle or the end of the word. Do not pronounce the words.

Reading
- Click the Reading tab for children to see the printed word. Note: Children *are not told* the word. The word is broken down into its constituent phonemes. Ask children to say each of the phonemes in the word.
- Click Blend to watch and hear the Bug's demonstration of how to blend the word.
- Click Undo and then ask a child to come to the Work area and move the arrow along. Encourage the whole class to blend the sounds out loud as the arrow moves along pushing the letters together. We recommend a smooth articulation of the sounds for blending.
- Work through each of the words in sequence. Click ▶ to change words.

Spelling
- The children return to their seats.
- Start by selecting the Words tab. Remember, the children do not see the word. Click Say to hear the word and ask the children to repeat it. Then ask the children to use their magnetic letters to make the word on their own magnetic boards, saying the word every time they look for a letter. Follow the procedure for word spelling on page 47.
- Ask a child to come up to the Work area to make the word. Did everyone get it right?
- Ask a child to use the arrow to push the letters together. Encourage the class to blend the word out loud.
- Repeat for the remaining word under the Words tab.
- Under the Pictures tab, click Show to display the image. You and the children say the picture word and proceed to spell it as before. Repeat if there is more than one image.

Writing
- Ask the children to find the 'n' letter among their magnetic letters and to feel the shape of it. Click Show and ask the children to look and listen as the lowercase letter is formed.
- "Skywrite" the letter in the air, and ask the children to do the same as you say how to form the letter.
- Ask children to tell you how to write the letter as you write it on the empty Work area.
- Ask children to try to write the letter themselves using paper and pencil or individual whiteboard and pen.
- Select uppercase and repeat when you think this to be appropriate for your children.

WRAP-UP
- Recap the learning intentions with the children.
- Play the "This is 'n'" video again, then play the alphabet song and encourage the children to sing along, signifying the end of the session.

Learning intentions are to:
- recap what we know
- say the /n/ phoneme
- find the letter 'n'
- read words with 'n' in
- spell words with 'n' in
- write the letter 'n'

Focus content: revision

Letters and Sounds
s, a, t, p, i
Reading
is, sip, sit, pips
Writing and Spelling
a, t, p, i
it, pip, pit, tip

Focus content: lesson

Sounds
"This is 'n'" video
Visual search
ant, pan, nap, Anna
Reading
Audio: pan, nap, nip, in
No audio: tan, Nan
Spelling
Words tab: an, pins
Pictures tab: pan, tins
Writing
n

Next steps
- Complete the PCM for Unit 2 (n)

Unit 2

Target phoneme /m/ written as 'm'

INTRODUCTION
- Play the alphabet song twice, once with voice accompaniment, children listening and singing along with accompaniment, and once with children singing along to the music without voice accompaniment.
- Discuss with the children the learning intentions for the day.

REVISION
[previously taught grapheme–phoneme correspondences; blending phonemes for reading; segmenting spoken words for spelling]
- Go through the Revision screens at a brisk pace.
- Watch out for any children who have not remembered the phonemes or the graphemes.

LESSON
Sounds
- Choose the relevant lesson session.
- Play the "This is 'm'" video once through.
- Say the phoneme /m/, and ask the children to repeat it after you. Make sure you keep the sound pure and encourage the children to do the same.

Visual Search
- Bring up the words from the asset bank onto the Work area. Ask the children to highlight the 'm' in each of the words, saying whether m's position is at the beginning, the middle or the end of the word. Do not pronounce the words.

Reading
- Click the Reading tab for children to see the printed word. Note: Children *are not told* the word. The word is broken down into its constituent phonemes. Ask children to say each of the phonemes in the word.
- Click Blend to watch and hear the Bug's demonstration of how to blend the word.
- Click Undo and then ask a child to come to the Work area and move the arrow along. Encourage the whole class to blend the sounds out loud as the arrow moves along pushing the letters together. We recommend a smooth articulation of the sounds for blending.
- Work through each of the words in sequence. Click ▶ to change words.

Spelling
- The children return to their seats.
- Start by selecting the Words tab. Remember, the children do not see the word. Click Say to hear the word and ask the children to repeat it. Then ask the children to use their magnetic letters to make the word on their own magnetic boards, saying the word every time they look for a letter. Follow the procedure for word spelling on page 47.
- Ask a child to come up to the Work area to make the word. Did everyone get it right?
- Ask a child to use the arrow to push the letters together. Encourage the class to blend the word out loud.
- Repeat for the remaining word under the Words tab.
- Under the Pictures tab, click Show to display the image. You and the children say the picture word and proceed to spell it as before. Repeat if there is more than one image.

Writing
- Ask the children to find the 'm' letter among their magnetic letters and to feel the shape of it. Click Show and ask the children to look and listen as the lowercase letter is formed.
- "Skywrite" the letter in the air, and ask the children to do the same as you say how to form the letter.
- Ask children to tell you how to write the letter as you write it on the empty Work area.
- Ask children to try to write the letter themselves using paper and pencil or individual whiteboard and pen.
- Select uppercase and repeat when you think this to be appropriate for your children.

WRAP-UP
- Recap the learning intentions with the children.
- Play the "This is 'm'" video again, then play the alphabet song and encourage the children to sing along, signifying the end of the session.

Learning intentions are to:
- recap what we know
- say the /m/ phoneme
- find the letter 'm'
- read words with 'm' in
- spell words with 'm' in
- write the letter 'm'

Focus content: revision

Letters and Sounds
s, a, t, p, i, n
Reading
an, pins, pan, tins
Writing and Spelling
t, p, i, n
tan, Nan, nip, in

Focus content: lesson

Sounds
"This is 'm'" video
Visual search
mint, stamp, pram, tramp
Reading
Audio: am, map, Sam, mats
No audio: mat, Pam
Spelling
Words tab: Tim, man
Pictures tab: mat, map
Writing
m

Next steps
- Complete the PCM for Unit 2 (m)

Unit 2

Target phoneme /d/ written as 'd'

INTRODUCTION
- Play the alphabet song twice, once with voice accompaniment, children listening and singing along with accompaniment, and once with children singing along to the music without voice accompaniment.
- Discuss with the children the learning intentions for the day.

REVISION
[previously taught grapheme–phoneme correspondences; blending phonemes for reading; segmenting spoken words for spelling]
- Go through the Revision screens at a brisk pace.
- Watch out for any children who have not remembered the phonemes or the graphemes.

LESSON
Sounds
- Choose the relevant lesson session.
- Play the "This is 'd'" video once through.
- Say the phoneme /d/, and ask the children to repeat it after you. Make sure you keep the sound pure and encourage the children to do the same.

Visual Search
- Bring up the words from the asset bank onto the Work area. Ask the children to highlight the 'd' in each of the words, saying whether d's position is at the beginning, the middle or the end of the word. Do not pronounce the words.

Reading
- Click the Reading tab for children to see the printed word. Note: Children *are not told* the word. The word is broken down into its constituent phonemes. Ask children to say each of the phonemes in the word.
- Click Blend to watch and hear the Bug's demonstration of how to blend the word.
- Click Undo and then ask a child to come to the Work area and move the arrow along. Encourage the whole class to blend the sounds out loud as the arrow moves along pushing the letters together. We recommend a smooth articulation of the sounds for blending.
- Work through each of the words in sequence. Click ▶ to change words.

Spelling
- The children return to their seats.
- Start by selecting the Words tab. Remember, the children do not see the word. Click Say to hear the word and ask the children to repeat it. Then ask the children to use their magnetic letters to make the word on their own magnetic boards, saying the word every time they look for a letter. Follow the procedure for word spelling on page 47.
- Ask a child to come up to the Work area to make the word. Did everyone get it right?
- Ask a child to use the arrow to push the letters together. Encourage the class to blend the word out loud.
- Repeat for the remaining word under the Words tab.
- Under the Pictures tab, click Show to display the image. You and the children say the picture word and proceed to spell it as before. Repeat if there is more than one image.
- Select the Spelling video and play it once through.

Writing
- Ask the children to find the 'd' letter among their magnetic letters and to feel the shape of it. Click Show and ask the children to look and listen as the lowercase letter is formed.
- "Skywrite" the letter in the air, and ask the children to do the same as you say how to form the letter.
- Ask children to tell you how to write the letter as you write it on the empty Work area.
- Ask children to try to write the letter themselves using paper and pencil or individual whiteboard and pen.
- Select uppercase and repeat when you think this to be appropriate for your children.

WRAP-UP
- Recap the learning intentions with the children.
- Play the "This is 'd'" video again, then play the alphabet song and encourage the children to sing along, signifying the end of the session.

Learning intentions are to:
- recap what we know
- say the /d/ phoneme
- find the letter 'd'
- read words with 'd' in
- spell words with 'd' in
- write the letter 'd'

Focus content: revision

Letters and Sounds
s, a, t, p, i, n, m
Reading
Tim, man, mat, map
Writing and Spelling
p, i, n, m
Sam, am, mats, Pam

Focus content: lesson

Sounds
"This is 'd'" video
Visual search
stand, damp, add, Adam
Reading
Audio: pad, dip, did, dim
No audio: mad, Sid
Spelling
Words tab: mad, Dan
Pictures tab: sad, Dad
Video: dim, damp
Writing
d

Next steps
- Complete the PCM for Unit 2 (d)

Unit 2

Language session

After: i, n, m, d

INTRODUCTION
- Play the alphabet song twice, once with voice accompaniment, children listening and singing along with accompaniment, and once with children singing along to the music without voice accompaniment.
- Discuss with the children the learning intentions for the day.

LESSON

Reading
- Click Show to display the words, and ask the children to read them.
- Click Answer to see whether they are right.
- Explain that 'i' is a vowel like 'a'.

Spelling
- Click Say to hear the caption and ask the children to repeat it.
- Ask the children to help you to select the lowercase magnetic letters and drag the letters to the empty boxes on the Work area.
- Ask the children to read the caption.
- Repeat the procedure for the remaining captions.

Writing
- The children return to their seats.
- Click Say to hear the caption and ask the children to repeat it.
- Ask the children to tell you how to write the caption on the lines provided.
- Clear the screen. Ask the children to say the caption and try to write it using paper and pencil or individual whiteboard and pen.
- Click Answer to check whether they are right.
- Repeat for the remaining captions.

Follow-up
- Display the picture. You and the children say the caption for the picture (a tin).
- Ask the children to spell the caption, using paper and pencil or magnetic letters.
- Click on the picture itself to show the caption.
- Ask the children to read the caption.

WRAP-UP
- Recap the learning intentions with the children.
- Play the alphabet song again and encourage the children to sing along, signifying the end of the session.

INTRODUCTION OF DECODABLE BOOKS
- Children have now learnt sufficient letter sounds to begin to read sentences in a story format.
- Unfamiliar words should be sounded and blended; do not suggest children use picture cues or guess from context.

> **Procedure for Teaching Irregular Words**
> Before the introduction of irregular words in the Unit 3 Language session, you may find this procedure for teaching irregular words helpful.
> - Set out the letters for the irregular word on the magnetic teaching board leaving a space between each of the letters.
> - Identify with the pupils any sounds/combination of sounds they may know which should help them to read the word.
> - Show the pupils how to read the irregular bit of the word.
> - Push the letters together from left to right with the children blending the sounds to say the word.
> - Replace the letters in the alphabet line.
> - Pronounce the word and ask the children to say how to spell the word as you write the letters on the board.
> - Read the written word.
> - When faced with an unknown irregular word in text, encourage the children to identify any known letter sounds/combination of sounds and think about what they know already before helping them to read the irregular bit and blend the sounds together to read the word.

Learning intentions are to:
- learn to read and spell short captions

Focus content: lesson

Reading
a tin, tin pins
Spelling
a pan, a pip, a mat
Writing
a pan, a pip, a mat
Follow-up
Picture shows: a tin

Next steps
- Play the online language pupil games for Unit 2
- Complete the language PCM for Unit 2
- Read Phonics Bug books that practise s, a, t, p, i, n, m, d:
  - In a Pit
  - It is a Din
  - Sid Did It
  - Sid's Nits
  - Sid's Pit
  - Tim's Din

Unit 3

Target phoneme /g/ written as 'g'

INTRODUCTION
- Play the alphabet song twice, once with voice accompaniment, children listening and singing along with accompaniment, and once with children singing along to the music without voice accompaniment.
- Discuss with the children the learning intentions for the day.

REVISION
[previously taught grapheme–phoneme correspondences; blending phonemes for reading; segmenting spoken words for spelling]
- Go through the Revision screens at a brisk pace.
- Watch out for any children who have not remembered the phonemes or the graphemes.

LESSON
Sounds
- Choose the relevant lesson session.
- Play the "This is 'g'" video once through.
- Say the phoneme /g/, and ask the children to repeat it after you. Make sure you keep the sound pure and encourage the children to do the same.

Visual Search
- Bring up the words from the asset bank onto the Work area. Ask the children to highlight the 'g' in each of the words, saying whether g's position is at the beginning, the middle or the end of the word. Do not pronounce the words.

Reading
- Click the Reading tab for children to see the printed word. Note: Children *are not told* the word. The word is broken down into its constituent phonemes. Ask children to say each of the phonemes in the word.
- Click Blend to watch and hear the Bug's demonstration of how to blend the word.
- Click Undo and then ask a child to come to the Work area and move the arrow along. Encourage the whole class to blend the sounds out loud as the arrow moves along pushing the letters together. We recommend a smooth articulation of the sounds for blending.
- Work through each of the words in sequence. Click ▶ to change words.

Spelling
- The children return to their seats.
- Start by selecting the Words tab. Remember, the children do not see the word. Click Say to hear the word and ask the children to repeat it. Then ask the children to use their magnetic letters to make the word on their own magnetic boards, saying the word every time they look for a letter. Follow the procedure for word spelling on page 47.
- Ask a child to come up to the Work area to make the word. Did everyone get it right?
- Ask a child to use the arrow to push the letters together. Encourage the class to blend the word out loud.
- Repeat for the remaining word under the Words tab.
- Under the Pictures tab, click Show to display the image. You and the children say the picture word and proceed to spell it as before. Repeat if there is more than one image.

Writing
- Ask the children to find the 'g' letter among their magnetic letters and to feel the shape of it. Click Show and ask the children to look and listen as the lowercase letter is formed.
- "Skywrite" the letter in the air, and ask the children to do the same as you say how to form the letter.
- Ask children to tell you how to write the letter as you write it on the empty Work area.
- Ask children to try to write the letter themselves using paper and pencil or individual whiteboard and pen.
- Select uppercase and repeat when you think this to be appropriate for your children.

WRAP-UP
- Recap the learning intentions with the children.
- Play the "This is 'g'" video again, then play the alphabet song and encourage the children to sing along, signifying the end of the session.

Learning intentions are to:
- recap what we know
- say the /g/ phoneme
- find the letter 'g'
- read words with 'g' in
- spell words with 'g' in
- write the letter 'g'

Focus content: revision

Letters and Sounds
s, a, t, p, i, n, m, d

Reading
mad, Dan, sad, Dad

Writing and Spelling
i, n, m, d
pad, dip, did, dim

Focus content: lesson

Sounds
"This is 'g'" video

Visual search

get, did, egg, grand

Reading
Audio: pig, gig, sag, gas
No audio: pigs, gag

Spelling
Words tab: gap, nag
Pictures tab: dig, tag

Writing
g

Next steps
- Play the online pupil games for Unit 2
- Complete the PCM for Unit 3 (g)
- Read Phonics Bug books that practise s, a, t, p, i, n, m, d:
   In a Pit
   It is a Din
   Sid Did It
   Sid's Nits
   Sid's Pit
   Tim's Din

Unit 3

Target phoneme /o/ written as 'o'

INTRODUCTION
- Play the alphabet song twice, once with voice accompaniment, children listening and singing along with accompaniment, and once with children singing along to the music without voice accompaniment.
- Discuss with the children the learning intentions for the day.

REVISION
[previously taught grapheme–phoneme correspondences; blending phonemes for reading; segmenting spoken words for spelling]
- Go through the Revision screens at a brisk pace.
- Watch out for any children who have not remembered the phonemes or the graphemes.

LESSON
Sounds
- Choose the relevant lesson session.
- Play the "This is 'o'" video once through.
- Say the phoneme /o/, and ask the children to repeat it after you. Make sure you keep the sound pure and encourage the children to do the same.

Visual Search
- Bring up the words from the asset bank onto the Work area. Ask the children to highlight the 'o' in each of the words, saying whether o's position is at the beginning, the middle or the end of the word. Do not pronounce the words.

Reading
- Click the Reading tab for children to see the printed word. Note: Children *are not told* the word. The word is broken down into its constituent phonemes. Ask children to say each of the phonemes in the word.
- Click Blend to watch and hear the Bug's demonstration of how to blend the word.
- Click Undo and then ask a child to come to the Work area and move the arrow along. Encourage the whole class to blend the sounds out loud as the arrow moves along pushing the letters together. We recommend a smooth articulation of the sounds for blending.
- Work through each of the words in sequence. Click ▶ to change words.

Spelling
- The children return to their seats.
- Start by selecting the Words tab. Remember, the children do not see the word. Click Say to hear the word and ask the children to repeat it. Then ask the children to use their magnetic letters to make the word on their own magnetic boards, saying the word every time they look for a letter. Follow the procedure for word spelling on page 47.
- Ask a child to come up to the Work area to make the word. Did everyone get it right?
- Ask a child to use the arrow to push the letters together. Encourage the class to blend the word out loud.
- Repeat for the remaining word under the Words tab.
- Under the Pictures tab, click Show to display the image. You and the children say the picture word and proceed to spell it as before. Repeat if there is more than one image.

Writing
- Ask the children to find the 'o' letter among their magnetic letters and to feel the shape of it. Click Show and ask the children to look and listen as the lowercase letter is formed.
- "Skywrite" the letter in the air, and ask the children to do the same as you say how to form the letter.
- Ask children to tell you how to write the letter as you write it on the empty Work area.
- Ask children to try to write the letter themselves using paper and pencil or individual whiteboard and pen.
- Select uppercase and repeat when you think this to be appropriate for your children.

WRAP-UP
- Recap the learning intentions with the children.
- Play the "This is 'o'" video again, then play the alphabet song and encourage the children to sing along, signifying the end of the session.

Learning intentions are to:
- recap what we know
- say the /o/ phoneme
- find the letter 'o'
- read words with 'o' in
- spell words with 'o' in
- write the letter 'o'

Focus content: revision

Letters and Sounds
a, t, p, i, n, m, d, g
Reading
gap, nag, dig, tag
Writing and Spelling
n, m, d, g
pig, gig, gas, gag

Focus content: lesson

Sounds
"This is 'o'" video
Visual search
pond, odd, lock, lollipop
Reading
Audio: on, pop, not, got
No audio: pots, nod
Spelling
Words tab: top, dot
Pictures tab: dog, mop
Writing
o

Next steps
- Play the online pupil games for Unit 2
- Complete the PCM for Unit 3 (o)
- Read Phonics Bug books that practise s, a, t, p, i, n, m, d:
    - In a Pit
    - It is a Din
    - Sid Did It
    - Sid's Nits
    - Sid's Pit
    - Tim's Din

Unit 3

Target phoneme /c/ written as 'c'

INTRODUCTION
- Play the alphabet song twice, once with voice accompaniment, children listening and singing along with accompaniment, and once with children singing along to the music without voice accompaniment.
- Discuss with the children the learning intentions for the day.

REVISION
[previously taught grapheme–phoneme correspondences; blending phonemes for reading; segmenting spoken words for spelling]
- Go through the Revision screens at a brisk pace.
- Watch out for any children who have not remembered the phonemes or the graphemes.

LESSON
Sounds
- Choose the relevant lesson session.
- Play the "This is 'c'" video once through.
- Say the phoneme /c/, and ask the children to repeat it after you. Make sure you keep the sound pure and encourage the children to do the same.

Visual Search
- Bring up the words from the asset bank onto the Work area. Ask the children to highlight the 'c' in each of the words, saying whether c's position is at the beginning, the middle or the end of the word. Do not pronounce the words.

Reading
- Click the Reading tab for children to see the printed word. Note: Children *are not told* the word. The word is broken down into its constituent phonemes. Ask children to say each of the phonemes in the word.
- Click Blend to watch and hear the Bug's demonstration of how to blend the word.
- Click Undo and then ask a child to come to the Work area and move the arrow along. Encourage the whole class to blend the sounds out loud as the arrow moves along pushing the letters together. We recommend a smooth articulation of the sounds for blending.
- Work through each of the words in sequence. Click ▶ to change words.

Spelling
- The children return to their seats.
- Start by selecting the Words tab. Remember, the children do not see the word. Click Say to hear the word and ask the children to repeat it. Then ask the children to use their magnetic letters to make the word on their own magnetic boards, saying the word every time they look for a letter. Follow the procedure for word spelling on page 47.
- Ask a child to come up to the Work area to make the word. Did everyone get it right?
- Ask a child to use the arrow to push the letters together. Encourage the class to blend the word out loud.
- Repeat for the remaining word under the Words tab.
- Under the Pictures tab, click Show to display the image. You and the children say the picture word and proceed to spell it as before. Repeat if there is more than one image.
- Select the Spelling video and play it once through.

Writing
- Ask the children to find the 'c' letter among their magnetic letters and to feel the shape of it. Click Show and ask the children to look and listen as the lowercase letter is formed.
- "Skywrite" the letter in the air, and ask the children to do the same as you say how to form the letter.
- Ask children to tell you how to write the letter as you write it on the empty Work area.
- Ask children to try to write the letter themselves using paper and pencil or individual whiteboard and pen.
- Select uppercase and repeat when you think this to be appropriate for your children.

WRAP-UP
- Recap the learning intentions with the children.
- Play the "This is 'c'" video again, then play the alphabet song and encourage the children to sing along, signifying the end of the session.

Learning intentions are to:
- recap what we know
- say the /c/ phoneme
- find the letter 'c'
- read words with 'c' in
- spell words with 'c' in
- write the letter 'c'

Focus content: revision

Letters and Sounds
t, p, i, n, m, d, g, o
Reading
on, dot, dog, mop
Writing and Spelling
m, d, g, o
pops, nod, top, got

Focus content: lesson

Sounds
"This is 'c'" video
Visual search
cap, act, cat, attic
Reading
Audio: cap, cat, cod, cog
No audio: cop, can
Spelling
Words tab: cot, cod
Pictures tab: cat, cap
Video: cot, can
Writing
c

Next steps
- Play the online pupil games for Unit 2
- Complete the PCM for Unit 3 (c)
- Read Phonics Bug books that practise s, a, t, p, i, n, m, d:
    In a Pit
    It is a Din
    Sid Did It
    Sid's Nits
    Sid's Pit
    Tim's Din

Unit 3

Target phoneme /c/ written as 'k'

INTRODUCTION
- Play the alphabet song twice, once with voice accompaniment, children listening and singing along with accompaniment, and once with children singing along to the music without voice accompaniment.
- Discuss with the children the learning intentions for the day.

REVISION
[previously taught grapheme–phoneme correspondences; blending phonemes for reading; segmenting spoken words for spelling]
- Go through the Revision screens at a brisk pace.
- Watch out for any children who have not remembered the phonemes or the graphemes.

LESSON
Sounds
- Choose the relevant lesson session.
- Play the "This is 'k'" video once through.
- Say the phoneme /c/, and ask the children to repeat it after you. Make sure you keep the sound pure and encourage the children to do the same.

Visual Search
- Bring up the words from the asset bank onto the Work area. Ask the children to highlight the 'k' in each of the words, saying whether k's position is at the beginning, the middle or the end of the word. Do not pronounce the words.

Reading
- Click the Reading tab for children to see the printed word. Note: Children *are not told* the word. The word is broken down into its constituent phonemes. Ask children to say each of the phonemes in the word.
- Click Blend to watch and hear the Bug's demonstration of how to blend the word.
- Click Undo and then ask a child to come to the Work area and move the arrow along. Encourage the whole class to blend the sounds out loud as the arrow moves along pushing the letters together. We recommend a smooth articulation of the sounds for blending.
- Work through each of the words in sequence. Click ▶ to change words.

Spelling
- The children return to their seats.
- Start by selecting the Words tab. Remember, the children do not see the word. Click Say to hear the word and ask the children to repeat it. Then ask the children to use their magnetic letters to make the word on their own magnetic boards, saying the word every time they look for a letter. Follow the procedure for word spelling on page 47.
- Ask a child to come up to the Work area to make the word. Did everyone get it right?
- Ask a child to use the arrow to push the letters together. Encourage the class to blend the word out loud.
- Repeat for the remaining word under the Words tab.
- Under the Pictures tab, click Show to display the image. You and the children say the picture word and proceed to spell it as before. Repeat if there is more than one image.

Writing
- Ask the children to find the 'k' letter among their magnetic letters and to feel the shape of it. Click Show and ask the children to look and listen as the lowercase letter is formed.
- "Skywrite" the letter in the air, and ask the children to do the same as you say how to form the letter.
- Ask children to tell you how to write the letter as you write it on the empty Work area.
- Ask children to try to write the letter themselves using paper and pencil or individual whiteboard and pen.
- Select uppercase and repeat when you think this to be appropriate for your children.

WRAP-UP
- Recap the learning intentions with the children.
- Play the "This is 'k'" video again, then play the alphabet song and encourage the children to sing along, signifying the end of the session.

Learning intentions are to:
- recap what we know
- say the /c/ phoneme
- find the letter 'k'
- read words with 'k' in
- spell words with 'k' in
- write the letter 'k'

Focus content: revision

Letters and Sounds
p, i, n, m, d, g, o, c
Reading
cot, cop, cat, cap
Writing and Spelling
d, g, o, c
cat, can, cod, cog

Focus content: lesson

Sounds
"This is 'k'" video
Visual search
desk, kiss, kept, Kent
Reading
Audio: kid, Kim, kit, kin
No audio: kids, kits
Spelling
Words tab: Kim, kin
Pictures tab: kids
Writing
k

Next steps
- Play the online pupil games for Unit 2
- Complete the PCM for Unit 3 (k)
- Read Phonics Bug books that practise s, a, t, p, i, n, m, d:
    In a Pit
    It is a Din
    Sid Did It
    Sid's Nits
    Sid's Pit
    Tim's Din

Unit 3

Language session

After: g, o, c, k

INTRODUCTION
- Play the alphabet song twice, once with voice accompaniment, children listening and singing along with accompaniment, and once with children singing along to the music without voice accompaniment.
- Discuss with the children the learning intentions for the day.

IRREGULAR

Reading
- Click Show to display the words, and ask/teach the children how to read them. Click Answer to hear the correct pronunciation.
- Explain that 'o' is a vowel like 'a' and 'i'. Point out that 'o' sounds /oo/ in this case.
*Although "and" is a regular word and should be easily sounded and blended at this stage, it is treated as not fully decodable here if adjacent consonants are not being taught until Phase 4. (See page 52 for more detail on the method for teaching the reading of irregular words.)

Spelling
- Click Say to hear the word and ask the children to repeat it.
- Put the word into a sentence, so that the children understand its meaning, for example, "I like apples and oranges", "I went to the shops".
- Ask children to say the word, help to select the lowercase magnetic letters and drag each letter into its empty box.
- Ask the children to read the word.
- Repeat for the remaining word.

LESSON

Reading
- Click Show to display the caption, and ask the children to read it.
- Click Answer to see whether they are right.
- Repeat for the second sentence. Explain that a sentence starts with a capital letter and ends with a full stop, e.g. "A cat is on a mat."

Spelling
- Click Say to hear the caption and ask the children to repeat it.
- Ask the children to help you to select the lowercase magnetic letters and drag the letters to the empty boxes on the Work area.
- Ask the children to read the caption.
- Repeat the procedure for the remaining captions.

Writing
- The children return to their seats.
- Click Say to hear the caption and ask the children to repeat it.
- Ask the children to tell you how to write the caption on the lines provided.
- Clear the screen. Ask the children to say the caption and try to write it using paper and pencil or individual whiteboard and pen.
- Click Answer to check whether they are right.
- Repeat for the remaining captions.

Follow-up
- Display the picture. You and the children say the word for the picture (kids).
- Ask the children to spell the word, using paper and pencil or magnetic letters.
- Click on the picture itself to show the word and ask the children to read it.

WRAP-UP
- Recap the learning intentions with the children.
- Play the alphabet song again and encourage the children to sing along, signifying the end of the session.

Learning intentions are to:
- learn to read and spell irregular words "and" and "to"
- learn to read and spell short captions

Focus content: irregular

Reading
and*, to

Spelling
and*, to

Focus content: lesson

Reading
a cat on a mat
Sam nods to Kim.

Spelling
a dog, on top, a sad man

Writing
a dog, on top, a sad man

Follow-up
Picture shows: kids

Next steps
- Play the online language pupil games for Unit 3
- Complete the language PCM for Unit 3
- Read Phonics Bug books that practise g, o, c, k:
    Cat and Dog
    Dig, Sid, Dig!
    Kat and Dan
    Kit and Dog
    Kit's Kip
    Pop! Pop! Pop!

Unit 4

Target phoneme /c/ written as 'ck'

INTRODUCTION
- Play the alphabet song twice, once with voice accompaniment, children listening and singing along with accompaniment, and once with children singing along to the music without voice accompaniment.
- Discuss with the children the learning intentions for the day.

REVISION
[previously taught grapheme–phoneme correspondences; blending phonemes for reading; segmenting spoken words for spelling]
- Go through the Revision screens at a brisk pace.
- Watch out for any children who have not remembered the phonemes or the graphemes.

LESSON

Sounds
- Choose the relevant lesson session.
- Play the "This is 'ck'" video once through.
- Say the phoneme /c/, and ask the children to repeat it after you. Make sure you keep the sound pure and encourage the children to do the same.
- Explain to the children that sometimes, two letters make one sound. Here, the letters 'c' and 'k' come together to make the sound /c/.

Visual Search
- Bring up the words from the asset bank onto the Work area. Ask the children to highlight the 'ck' in each of the words, saying whether ck's position is at the beginning, the middle or the end of the word. Do not pronounce the words.

Reading
- Click the Reading tab for children to see the printed word. Note: Children *are not told* the word. The word is broken down into its constituent phonemes. Ask children to say each of the phonemes in the word.
- Click Blend to watch and hear the Bug's demonstration of how to blend the word.
- Click Undo and then ask a child to come to the Work area and move the arrow along. Encourage the whole class to blend the sounds out loud as the arrow moves along pushing the letters together. We recommend a smooth articulation of the sounds for blending.
- Work through each of the words in sequence. Click ▶ to change words.

Spelling
- The children return to their seats.
- Start by selecting the Words tab. Remember, the children do not see the word. Click Say to hear the word and ask the children to repeat it. Then ask the children to use their magnetic letters to make the word on their own magnetic boards, saying the word every time they look for a letter. Follow the procedure for word spelling on page 47.
- Ask a child to come up to the Work area to make the word. Did everyone get it right?
- Ask a child to use the arrow to push the letters together. Encourage the class to blend the word out loud.
- Repeat for the remaining word under the Words tab.
- Under the Pictures tab, click Show to display the image. You and the children say the picture word and proceed to spell it as before. Repeat if there is more than one image.

Writing
- Ask the children to find the 'c' and 'k' letters among their magnetic letters and to feel the shape of them. Click Show and ask the children to look and listen as the lowercase letters are formed.
- "Skywrite" the letters in the air, and ask the children to do the same as you say how to form the letters.
- Ask children to tell you how to write the letters as you write them on the empty Work area.
- Ask children to try to write the letters themselves using paper and pencil or individual whiteboard and pen.
- Select uppercase and repeat when you think this to be appropriate for your children.

WRAP-UP
- Recap the learning intentions with the children.
- Play the "This is 'ck'" video again, then play the alphabet song and encourage the children to sing along, signifying the end of the session.

Learning intentions are to:
- recap what we know
- say the /c/ phoneme
- find the letters 'ck'
- read words with 'ck' in
- spell words with 'ck' in
- write the letters 'ck'

Focus content: revision

Letters and Sounds
i, n, m, d, g, o, c, k
Reading
Kim, kin, kids, kits
Writing and Spelling
g, o, c, k
kid, Kim, kit, kin

Focus content: lesson

Sounds
"This is 'ck'" video
Visual search
neck, packet, ticket, Mick
Reading
Audio: Mick, sock, sick, dock
No audio: kick, pack, pick, tack
Spelling
Words tab: picks, mock
Pictures tab: sack, tick
Writing
ck

Next steps
- Play the online pupil games for Unit 3
- Complete the PCM for Unit 4 (ck)
- Read Phonics Bug books that practise g, o, c, k:
  - Cat and Dog
  - Dig, Sid, Dig!
  - Kat and Dan
  - Kit and Dog
  - Kit's Kip
  - Pop! Pop! Pop!

Unit 4

Target phoneme /e/ written as 'e'

INTRODUCTION
- Play the alphabet song twice, once with voice accompaniment, children listening and singing along with accompaniment, and once with children singing along to the music without voice accompaniment.
- Discuss with the children the learning intentions for the day.

REVISION
[previously taught grapheme–phoneme correspondences; blending phonemes for reading; segmenting spoken words for spelling]
- Go through the Revision screens at a brisk pace.
- Watch out for any children who have not remembered the phonemes or the graphemes.

LESSON

Sounds
- Choose the relevant lesson session.
- Play the "This is 'e'" video once through.
- Say the phoneme /e/, and ask the children to repeat it after you. Make sure you keep the sound pure and encourage the children to do the same.

Visual Search
- Bring up the words from the asset bank onto the Work area. Ask the children to highlight the 'e' in each of the words, saying whether e's position is at the beginning, the middle or the end of the word. Do not pronounce the words.

Reading
- Click the Reading tab for children to see the printed word. Note: Children *are not told* the word. The word is broken down into its constituent phonemes. Ask children to say each of the phonemes in the word.
- Click Blend to watch and hear the Bug's demonstration of how to blend the word.
- Click Undo and then ask a child to come to the Work area and move the arrow along. Encourage the whole class to blend the sounds out loud as the arrow moves along pushing the letters together. We recommend a smooth articulation of the sounds for blending.
- Work through each of the words in sequence. Click ▶ to change words.

Spelling
- The children return to their seats.
- Start by selecting the Words tab. Remember, the children do not see the word. Click Say to hear the word and ask the children to repeat it. Then ask the children to use their magnetic letters to make the word on their own magnetic boards, saying the word every time they look for a letter. Follow the procedure for word spelling on page 47.
- Ask a child to come up to the Work area to make the word. Did everyone get it right?
- Ask a child to use the arrow to push the letters together. Encourage the class to blend the word out loud.
- Repeat for the remaining word under the Words tab.
- Under the Pictures tab, click Show to display the image. You and the children say the picture word and proceed to spell it as before. Repeat if there is more than one image.

Writing
- Ask the children to find the 'e' letter among their magnetic letters and to feel the shape of it. Click Show and ask the children to look and listen as the lowercase letter is formed.
- "Skywrite" the letter in the air, and ask the children to do the same as you say how to form the letter.
- Ask children to tell you how to write the letter as you write it on the empty Work area.
- Ask children to try to write the letter themselves using paper and pencil or individual whiteboard and pen.
- Select uppercase and repeat when you think this to be appropriate for your children.

WRAP-UP
- Recap the learning intentions with the children.
- Play the "This is 'e'" video again, then play the alphabet song and encourage the children to sing along, signifying the end of the session.

Learning intentions are to:
- recap what we know
- say the /e/ phoneme
- find the letter 'e'
- read words with 'e' in
- spell words with 'e' in
- write the letter 'e'

Focus content: revision

Letters and Sounds
n, m, d, g, o, c, k, ck
Reading
picks, mock, sack, tick
Writing and Spelling
o, c, k, ck
kick, pack, pick, tack

Focus content: lesson

Sounds
"This is 'e'" video
Visual search
end, test, spend, Emma
Reading
Audio: pet, neck, ten, egg
No audio: men, get, deck, peck
Spelling
Words tab: den, met
Pictures tab: pen, peg
Writing
e

Next steps
- Play the online pupil games for Unit 3
- Complete the PCM for Unit 4 (e)
- Read Phonics Bug books that practise g, o, c, k:
    Cat and Dog
    Dig, Sid, Dig!
    Kat and Dan
    Kit and Dog
    Kit's Kip
    Pop! Pop! Pop!

Unit 4

Target phoneme /u/ written as 'u'

INTRODUCTION
- Play the alphabet song twice, once with voice accompaniment, children listening and singing along with accompaniment, and once with children singing along to the music without voice accompaniment.
- Discuss with the children the learning intentions for the day.

REVISION
[previously taught grapheme–phoneme correspondences; blending phonemes for reading; segmenting spoken words for spelling]
- Go through the Revision screens at a brisk pace.
- Watch out for any children who have not remembered the phonemes or the graphemes.

LESSON

Sounds
- Choose the relevant lesson session.
- Play the "This is 'u'" video once through.
- Say the phoneme /u/, and ask the children to repeat it after you. Make sure you keep the sound pure and encourage the children to do the same.
- If appropriate, explain the regional variation in the way the 'u' sound in words such as "cut" and "bus" is pronounced.

Visual Search
- Bring up the words from the asset bank onto the Work area. Ask the children to highlight the 'u' in each of the words, saying whether u's position is at the beginning, the middle or the end of the word. Do not pronounce the words.

Reading
- Click the Reading tab for children to see the printed word. Note: Children *are not told* the word. The word is broken down into its constituent phonemes. Ask children to say each of the phonemes in the word.
- Click Blend to watch and hear the Bug's demonstration of how to blend the word.
- Click Undo and then ask a child to come to the Work area and move the arrow along. Encourage the whole class to blend the sounds out loud as the arrow moves along pushing the letters together. We recommend a smooth articulation of the sounds for blending.
- Work through each of the words in sequence. Click ▶ to change words.

Spelling
- The children return to their seats.
- Start by selecting the Words tab. Remember, the children do not see the word. Click Say to hear the word and ask the children to repeat it. Then ask the children to use their magnetic letters to make the word on their own magnetic boards, saying the word every time they look for a letter. Follow the procedure for word spelling on page 47.
- Ask a child to come up to the Work area to make the word. Did everyone get it right?
- Ask a child to use the arrow to push the letters together. Encourage the class to blend the word out loud.
- Repeat for the remaining word under the Words tab.
- Under the Pictures tab, click Show to display the image. You and the children say the picture word and proceed to spell it as before. Repeat if there is more than one image.

Writing
- Ask the children to find the 'u' letter among their magnetic letters and to feel the shape of it. Click Show and ask the children to look and listen as the lowercase letter is formed.
- "Skywrite" the letter in the air, and ask the children to do the same as you say how to form the letter.
- Ask children to tell you how to write the letter as you write it on the empty Work area.
- Ask children to try to write the letter themselves using paper and pencil or individual whiteboard and pen.
- Select uppercase and repeat when you think this to be appropriate for your children.

WRAP-UP
- Recap the learning intentions with the children.
- Play the "This is 'u'" video again, then play the alphabet song and encourage the children to sing along, signifying the end of the session.

Learning intentions are to:
- recap what we know
- say the /u/ phoneme
- find the letter 'u'
- read words with 'u' in
- spell words with 'u' in
- write the letter 'u'

Focus content: revision

Letters and Sounds
m, d, g, o, c, k, ck, e
Reading
den, met, pen, peg
Writing and Spelling
c, k, ck, e
men, get, deck, peck

Focus content: lesson

Sounds
"This is 'u'" video
Visual search
slug, upon, jump, but
Reading
Audio: up, Mum, nut, duck
No audio: us, cut, mug, suck
Spelling
Words tab: sum, mud
Pictures tab: cup, sun
Writing
u

Next steps
- Play the online pupil games for Unit 3
- Complete the PCM for Unit 4 (u)
- Read Phonics Bug books that practise g, o, c, k:
    - Cat and Dog
    - Dig, Sid, Dig!
    - Kat and Dan
    - Kit and Dog
    - Kit's Kip
    - Pop! Pop! Pop!

Unit 4

Target phoneme /r/ written as 'r'

INTRODUCTION
- Play the alphabet song twice, once with voice accompaniment, children listening and singing along with accompaniment, and once with children singing along to the music without voice accompaniment.
- Discuss with the children the learning intentions for the day.

REVISION
[previously taught grapheme–phoneme correspondences; blending phonemes for reading; segmenting spoken words for spelling]
- Go through the Revision screens at a brisk pace.
- Watch out for any children who have not remembered the phonemes or the graphemes.

LESSON

Sounds
- Choose the relevant lesson session.
- Play the "This is 'r'" video once through.
- Say the phoneme /r/, and ask the children to repeat it after you. Make sure you keep the sound pure and encourage the children to do the same.

Visual Search
- Bring up the words from the asset bank onto the Work area. Ask the children to highlight the 'r' in each of the words, saying whether r's position is at the beginning, the middle or the end of the word. Do not pronounce the words.

Reading
- Click the Reading tab for children to see the printed word. Note: Children *are not told* the word. The word is broken down into its constituent phonemes. Ask children to say each of the phonemes in the word.
- Click Blend to watch and hear the Bug's demonstration of how to blend the word.
- Click Undo and then ask a child to come to the Work area and move the arrow along. Encourage the whole class to blend the sounds out loud as the arrow moves along pushing the letters together. We recommend a smooth articulation of the sounds for blending.
- Work through each of the words in sequence. Click ▶ to change words.

Spelling
- The children return to their seats.
- Start by selecting the Words tab. Remember, the children do not see the word. Click Say to hear the word and ask the children to repeat it. Then ask the children to use their magnetic letters to make the word on their own magnetic boards, saying the word every time they look for a letter. Follow the procedure for word spelling on page 47.
- Ask a child to come up to the Work area to make the word. Did everyone get it right?
- Ask a child to use the arrow to push the letters together. Encourage the class to blend the word out loud.
- Repeat for the remaining word under the Words tab.
- Under the Pictures tab, click Show to display the image. You and the children say the picture word and proceed to spell it as before. Repeat if there is more than one image.
- Select the Spelling video and play it once through.

Writing
- Ask the children to find the 'r' letter among their magnetic letters and to feel the shape of it. Click Show and ask the children to look and listen as the lowercase letter is formed.
- "Skywrite" the letter in the air, and ask the children to do the same as you say how to form the letter.
- Ask children to tell you how to write the letter as you write it on the empty Work area.
- Ask children to try to write the letter themselves using paper and pencil or individual whiteboard and pen.
- Select uppercase and repeat when you think this to be appropriate for your children.

WRAP-UP
- Recap the learning intentions with the children.
- Play the "This is 'r'" video again, then play the alphabet song and encourage the children to sing along, signifying the end of the session.

Learning intentions are to:
- recap what we know
- say the /r/ phoneme
- find the letter 'r'
- read words with 'r' in
- spell words with 'r' in
- write the letter 'r'

Focus content: revision

Letters and Sounds
d, g, o, c, k, ck, e, u
Reading
sum, mud, cup, sun
Writing and Spelling
k, ck, e, u
us, cut, mug, suck

Focus content: lesson

Sounds
"This is 'r'" video
Visual search
trip, rat, rap, print
Reading
Audio: run, rag, rut, rim
No audio: rap, rug, rid, rock
Spelling
Words tab: ran, red
Pictures tab: rat, rod
Video: rip, red
Writing
r

Next steps
- Play the online pupil games for Unit 3
- Complete the PCM for Unit 4 (r)
- Read Phonics Bug books that practise g, o, c, k:
  - Cat and Dog
  - Dig, Sid, Dig!
  - Kat and Dan
  - Kit and Dog
  - Kit's Kip
  - Pop! Pop! Pop!

Unit 4

Language session

After: ck, e, u, r

INTRODUCTION
- Play the alphabet song twice, once with voice accompaniment, children listening and singing along with accompaniment, and once with children singing along to the music without voice accompaniment.
- Discuss with the children the learning intentions for the day.

IRREGULAR

Reading
- Click Show to display the words, and ask/teach the children how to read them. Click Answer to hear the correct pronunciation. Ask the children to repeat it.
- Explain that 'e' and 'u' are vowels like 'a', 'i', and 'o'.
- ⓘ If 'the' is being used before a word beginning with a consonant, the 'e' sounds a short /e/; if it is being used before a word beginning with a vowel, the 'e' sounds /ee/. Depending on the geographical region you are in, the 'e' can also sound /i/.
- In the words 'no' and 'go', 'o' sounds like its letter name, pronounced /oa/.

Spelling
- Click Say to hear the word, and ask the children to repeat it.
- Put the word into a sentence, so that the children understand its meaning, for example, "Close the door", "There were no sweets left", "Let's go to the park".
- Ask children to say the word, help to select the lowercase magnetic letters and drag each letter into its empty box.
- Ask the children to read the word.
- Repeat for the remaining words.

LESSON

Reading
- Click Show to display the caption, and ask the children to read it.
- Click Answer to see whether they are right.
- Repeat for the sentence. Remind the children that a sentence starts with a capital letter and ends with a full stop.

Spelling
- Click Say to hear the caption and ask the children to repeat it.
- Ask the children to help you to select the lowercase magnetic letters and drag the letters to the empty boxes on the Work area.
- Ask the children to read the caption.
- Repeat the procedure for the remaining captions.

Writing
- The children return to their seats.
- Click Say to hear the caption and ask the children to repeat it.
- Ask the children to tell you how to write the caption on the lines provided.
- Clear the screen. Ask the children to say the caption and try to write it using paper and pencil or individual whiteboard and pen.
- Click Answer to check whether they are right.
- Repeat for the remaining captions.

Follow-up
- Display the picture. You and the children say the caption for the picture (a red pen).
- Ask the children to spell the caption, using pencil and paper.
- Click on the picture itself to show the caption and ask the children to read it.

WRAP-UP
- Recap the learning intentions with the children.
- Play the alphabet song again and encourage the children to sing along, signifying the end of the session.

Learning intentions are to:
- learn to read and spell irregular words "the", "no" and "go"
- learn to read and spell short captions

Focus content: irregular

Reading
the, no, go
Spelling
the, no, go

Focus content: lesson

Reading
no pets in the den
Mick and Ken go to get nuts.
Spelling
a mug, ten men, run in the sun
Writing
a mug, ten men, run in the sun
Follow-up
Picture shows: a red pen

Next steps
- Play the online language pupil games for Unit 4
- Complete the language PCM for Unit 4
- Read Phonics Bug books that practise ck, e, u, r:
  - Get a Pet!
  - In the Pit
  - Is it a Rock?
  - Sid and Duck
  - Sid's Pet Rat
  - Tut, Tut, Pup!

Unit 5

Target phoneme /h/ written as 'h'

INTRODUCTION
- Play the alphabet song twice, once with voice accompaniment, children listening and singing along with accompaniment, and once with children singing along to the music without voice accompaniment.
- Discuss with the children the learning intentions for the day.

REVISION
[previously taught grapheme–phoneme correspondences; blending phonemes for reading; segmenting spoken words for spelling]
- Go through the Revision screens at a brisk pace.
- Watch out for any children who have not remembered the phonemes or the graphemes.

LESSON
Sounds
- Choose the relevant lesson session.
- Play the "This is 'h'" video once through.
- Say the phoneme /h/, and ask the children to repeat it after you. Make sure you keep the sound pure and encourage the children to do the same.

Visual Search
- Bring up the words from the asset bank onto the Work area. Ask the children to highlight the 'h' in each of the words, saying whether h's position is at the beginning, the middle or the end of the word. Do not pronounce the words.

Reading
- Click the Reading tab for children to see the printed word. Note: Children *are not told* the word. The word is broken down into its constituent phonemes. Ask children to say each of the phonemes in the word.
- Click Blend to watch and hear the Bug's demonstration of how to blend the word.
- Click Undo and then ask a child to come to the Work area and move the arrow along. Encourage the whole class to blend the sounds out loud as the arrow moves along pushing the letters together. We recommend a smooth articulation of the sounds for blending.
- Work through each of the words in sequence. Click ▶ to change words.

Spelling
- The children return to their seats.
- Start by selecting the Words tab. Remember, the children do not see the word. Click Say to hear the word and ask the children to repeat it. Then ask the children to use their magnetic letters to make the word on their own magnetic boards, saying the word every time they look for a letter. Follow the procedure for word spelling on page 47.
- Ask a child to come up to the Work area to make the word. Did everyone get it right?
- Ask a child to use the arrow to push the letters together. Encourage the class to blend the word out loud.
- Repeat for the remaining word under the Words tab.
- Under the Pictures tab, click Show to display the image. You and the children say the picture word and proceed to spell it as before. Repeat if there is more than one image.
- Select the Spelling video and play it once through.

Writing
- Ask the children to find the 'h' letter among their magnetic letters and to feel the shape of it. Click Show and ask the children to look and listen as the lowercase letter is formed.
- "Skywrite" the letter in the air, and ask the children to do the same as you say how to form the letter.
- Ask children to tell you how to write the letter as you write it on the empty Work area.
- Ask children to try to write the letter themselves using paper and pencil or individual whiteboard and pen.
- Select uppercase and repeat when you think this to be appropriate for your children.

WRAP-UP
- Recap the learning intentions with the children.
- Play the "This is 'h'" video again, then play the alphabet song and encourage the children to sing along, signifying the end of the session.

Learning intentions are to:
- recap what we know
- say the /h/ phoneme
- find the letter 'h'
- read words with 'h' in
- spell words with 'h' in
- write the letter 'h'

Focus content: revision

Letters and Sounds
g, o, c, k, ck, e, u, r

Reading
ran, red, rat, rod

Writing and Spelling
ck, e, u, r
rap, rug, rid, rock

Focus content: lesson

Sounds
"This is 'h'" video

Visual search
huff, hand, uphill, Helen

Reading
Audio: hop, hem, his, has
No audio: him, hut, had, hid

Spelling
Words tab: hot, hug
Pictures tab: hens, hat
Video: hen, ham

Writing
h

Next steps
- Play the online pupil games for Unit 4
- Complete the PCM for Unit 5 (h)
- Read Phonics Bug books that practise ck, e, u, r:
  - Get a Pet!
  - In the Pit
  - Is it a Rock?
  - Sid and Duck
  - Sid's Pet Rat
  - Tut, Tut, Pup!

Unit 5

Target phoneme /b/ written as 'b'

INTRODUCTION
- Play the alphabet song twice, once with voice accompaniment, children listening and singing along with accompaniment, and once with the children singing along to the music without voice accompaniment.
- Discuss with the children the learning intentions for the day.

REVISION
[previously taught grapheme–phoneme correspondences; blending phonemes for reading; segmenting spoken words for spelling]
- Go through the Revision screens at a brisk pace.
- Watch out for any children who have not remembered the phonemes or the graphemes.

LESSON

Sounds
- Choose the relevant lesson session.
- Play the "This is 'b'" video once through.
- Say the phoneme /b/, and ask the children to repeat it after you. Make sure you keep the sound pure and encourage the children to do the same.

Visual Search
- Bring up the words from the asset bank onto the Work area. Ask the children to highlight the 'b' in each of the words, saying whether b's position is at the beginning, the middle or the end of the word. Do not pronounce the words.

Reading
- Click the Reading tab for children to see the printed word. Note: Children *are not told* the word. The word is broken down into its constituent phonemes. Ask children to say each of the phonemes in the word.
- Click Blend to watch and hear the Bug's demonstration of how to blend the word.
- Click Undo and then ask a child to come to the Work area and move the arrow along. Encourage the whole class to blend the sounds out loud as the arrow moves along pushing the letters together. We recommend a smooth articulation of the sounds for blending.
- Work through each of the words in sequence. Click ▶ to change words.

Spelling
- The children return to their seats.
- Start by selecting the Words tab. Remember, the children do not see the word. Click Say to hear the word and ask the children to repeat it. Then ask the children to use their magnetic letters to make the word on their own magnetic boards, saying the word every time they look for a letter. Follow the procedure for word spelling on page 47.
- Ask a child to come up to the Work area to make the word. Did everyone get it right?
- Ask a child to use the arrow to push the letters together. Encourage the class to blend the word out loud.
- Repeat for the remaining word under the Words tab.
- Under the Pictures tab, click Show to display the image. You and the children say the picture word and proceed to spell it as before. Repeat if there is more than one image.

Writing
- Ask the children to find the 'b' letter among their magnetic letters and to feel the shape of it. Click Show and ask the children to look and listen as the lowercase letter is formed.
- "Skywrite" the letter in the air, and ask the children to do the same as you say how to form the letter.
- Ask children to tell you how to write the letter as you write it on the empty Work area.
- Ask children to try to write the letter themselves using paper and pencil or individual whiteboard and pen.
- Select uppercase and repeat when you think this to be appropriate for your children.

WRAP-UP
- Recap the learning intentions with the children.
- Play the "This is 'b'" video again, then play the alphabet song and encourage the children to sing along, signifying the end of the session.

Learning intentions are to:
- recap what we know
- say the /b/ phoneme
- find the letter 'b'
- read words with 'b' in
- spell words with 'b' in
- write the letter 'b'

Focus content: revision

Letters and Sounds
o, c, k, ck, e, u, r, h
Reading
hot, hug, hens, hat
Writing and Spelling
e, u, r, h
him, hut, had, hid

Focus content: lesson

Sounds
"This is 'b'" video
Visual search
crab, belt, blob, rabbit
Reading
Audio: bad, but, Bob, back
No audio: bat, bed, rub, cabin
Spelling
Words tab: rib, big
Pictures tab: bag, bus
Writing
b

Next steps
- Play the online pupil games for Unit 4
- Complete the PCM for Unit 5 (b)
- Read Phonics Bug books that practise ck, e, u, r:
  - Get a Pet!
  - In the Pit
  - Is it a Rock?
  - Sid and Duck
  - Sid's Pet Rat
  - Tut, Tut, Pup!

Unit 5

Target phoneme /f/ written as 'f' and 'ff'

INTRODUCTION
- Play the alphabet song twice, once with voice accompaniment, children listening and singing along with accompaniment, and once with children singing along to the music without voice accompaniment.
- Discuss with the children the learning intentions for the day.

REVISION
[previously taught grapheme–phoneme correspondences; blending phonemes for reading; segmenting spoken words for spelling]
- Go through the Revision screens at a brisk pace.
- Remind the children about the concept of two letters making one sound, e.g. 'ck' in 'back'.
- Watch out for any children who have not remembered the phonemes or the graphemes.

LESSON
Sounds
- Choose the relevant lesson session.
- Play the "This is 'f'" video once through.
- Say the phoneme /f/, and ask the children to repeat it after you. Make sure you keep the sound pure and encourage the children to do the same.

Visual Search
- Bring up the words from the asset bank onto the Work area. Ask the children to highlight the 'f' or 'ff' in each of the words, saying whether the positions of 'f' and 'ff' are at the beginning, the middle or the end of the word. Do not pronounce the words.

Reading
- Click the Reading tab for children to see the printed word. Note: Children *are not told* the word. The word is broken down into its constituent phonemes. Ask children to say each of the phonemes in the word.
- Click Blend to watch and hear the Bug's demonstration of how to blend the word.
- Click Undo and then ask a child to come to the Work area and move the arrow along. Encourage the whole class to blend the sounds out loud as the arrow moves along pushing the letters together. We recommend a smooth articulation of the sounds for blending.
- Work through each of the words in sequence. Click ▶ to change words.

Spelling
- The children return to their seats.
- Start by selecting the Words tab. Remember, the children do not see the word. Click Say to hear the word and ask the children to repeat it. Then ask the children to use their magnetic letters to make the word on their own magnetic boards, saying the word every time they look for a letter. Follow the procedure for word spelling on page 47.
- Ask a child to come up to the Work area to make the word. Did everyone get it right?
- Ask a child to use the arrow to push the letters together. Encourage the class to blend the word out loud.
- Repeat for the remaining word under the Words tab.
- Under the Pictures tab, click Show to display the image. You and the children say the picture word and proceed to spell it as before. Repeat if there is more than one image.

Writing
- Ask the children to find the 'f' letter among their magnetic letters and to feel the shape of it. Click Show and ask the children to look and listen as the lowercase letter is formed.
- "Skywrite" the letter(s) in the air, and ask the children to do the same as you say how to form the letter.
- Ask children to tell you how to write the letter(s) as you write it (them) on the empty Work area.
- Ask children to try to write the letter(s) themselves using paper and pencil or individual whiteboard and pen.
- Select uppercase and repeat when you think this to be appropriate for your children.

WRAP-UP
- Recap the learning intentions with the children.
- Play the "This is 'f'" video again, then play the alphabet song and encourage the children to sing along, signifying the end of the session.

Learning intentions are to:
- recap what we know
- say the /f/ phoneme
- find 'f' and 'ff' in words
- read words with 'f' and 'ff' in
- spell words with 'f' and 'ff' in
- write the letter 'f'

Focus content: revision

Letters and Sounds
c, k, ck, e, u, r, h, b

Reading
rib, big, bag, bus

Writing and Spelling
u, r, h, b
bad, bed, rub, cabin

Focus content: lesson

Sounds
"This is 'f'" video

Visual search
flag, left, sniff, Fred

Reading
Audio: of, fog, fig, off
No audio: if, fit, fib, cuff

Spelling
Words tab: fun, puff
Pictures tab: fan, fin

Writing
f, ff

Next steps
- Play the online pupil games for Unit 4
- Complete the PCM for Unit 5 (f)
- Read Phonics Bug books that practise ck, e, u, r:
  Get a Pet!
  In the Pit
  Is it a Rock?
  Sid and Duck
  Sid's Pet Rat
  Tut, Tut, Pup!

Unit 5

Target phoneme /l/ written as 'l' and 'll'

INTRODUCTION
- Play the alphabet song twice, once with voice accompaniment, children listening and singing along with accompaniment, and once with children singing along to the music without voice accompaniment.
- Discuss with the children the learning intentions for the day.

REVISION
[previously taught grapheme–phoneme correspondences; blending phonemes for reading; segmenting spoken words for spelling]
- Remind the children about the concept of two letters making one sound, e.g. 'ff' in 'puff'.
- Watch out for any children who have not remembered the phonemes or the graphemes.

LESSON

Sounds
- Choose the relevant lesson session.
- Play the "This is 'l'" video once through.
- Say the phoneme /l/, and ask the children to repeat it after you. Make sure you keep the sound pure and encourage the children to do the same.

Visual Search
- Bring up the words from the asset bank onto the Work area. Ask the children to highlight the 'l' or 'll' in each of the words, saying whether the position of 'l' or 'll' is at the beginning, the middle or the end of the word. Do not pronounce the words.

Reading
- Click the Reading tab for children to see the printed word. Note: Children *are not told* the word. The word is broken down into its constituent phonemes. Ask children to say each of the phonemes in the word.
- Click Blend to watch and hear the Bug's demonstration of how to blend the word.
- Click Undo and then ask a child to come to the Work area and move the arrow along. Encourage the whole class to blend the sounds out loud as the arrow moves along pushing the letters together. We recommend a smooth articulation of the sounds for blending.
- Work through each of the words in sequence. Click ▶ to change words.

Spelling
- The children return to their seats.
- Start by selecting the Words tab. Remember, the children do not see the word. Click Say to hear the word and ask the children to repeat it. Then ask the children to use their magnetic letters to make the word on their own magnetic boards, saying the word every time they look for a letter. Follow the procedure for word spelling on page 47.
- Ask a child to come up to the Work area to make the word. Did everyone get it right?
- Ask a child to use the arrow to push the letters together. Encourage the class to blend the word out loud.
- Repeat for the remaining word under the Words tab.
- Under the Pictures tab, click Show to display the image. You and the children say the picture word and proceed to spell it as before. Repeat if there is more than one image.

Writing
- Ask the children to find the 'l' letter among their magnetic letters and to feel the shape of it. Click Show and ask the children to look and listen as the lowercase letter is formed.
- "Skywrite" the letter(s) in the air, and ask the children to do the same as you say how to form the letter.
- Ask children to tell you how to write the letter(s) as you write it (them) on the empty Work area.
- Ask children to try to write the letter(s) themselves using paper and pencil or individual whiteboard and pen.
- Select uppercase and repeat when you think this to be appropriate for your children.

WRAP-UP
- Recap the learning intentions with the children.
- Play the "This is 'l'" video again, then play the alphabet song and encourage the children to sing along, signifying the end of the session.

Learning intentions are to:
- recap what we know
- say the /l/ phoneme
- find 'l' and 'll' in words
- read words with 'l' and 'll' in
- spell words with 'l' and 'll' in
- write the letter 'l'

Focus content: revision

Letters and Sounds
k, ck, e, u, r, h, b, f, ff
Reading
fun, puff, fan, fin
Writing and Spelling
r, h, b, f, ff
if, fit, fib, cuff

Focus content: lesson

Sounds
"This is 'l'" video
Visual search
spell, leg, land, milk
Reading
Audio: lip, lot, lick, bell
No audio: lock, sell, dull, laptop
Spelling
Words tab: let, tell
Pictures tab: leg, doll
Writing
l, ll

Next steps
- Play the online pupil games for Unit 4
- Complete the PCM for Unit 5 (l)
- Read Phonics Bug books that practise ck, e, u, r:
  - Get a Pet!
  - In the Pit
  - Is it a Rock?
  - Sid and Duck
  - Sid's Pet Rat
  - Tut, Tut, Pup!

Unit 5

Target phoneme /s/ written as 'ss'

INTRODUCTION
- Play the alphabet song twice, once with voice accompaniment, children listening and singing along with accompaniment, and once with children singing along to the music without voice accompaniment.
- Discuss with the children the learning intentions for the day.

REVISION
[previously taught grapheme–phoneme correspondences; blending phonemes for reading; segmenting spoken words for spelling]
- Go through the Revision screens at a brisk pace.
- Remind the children about the concept of two letters making one sound, e.g. 'll' in "bell".
- Watch out for any children who have not remembered the phonemes or the graphemes.

LESSON
Sounds
- Choose the relevant lesson session.
- Play the "This is 'ss'" video once through.
- Say the phoneme /s/, and ask the children to repeat it after you. Make sure you keep the sound pure and encourage the children to do the same.

Visual Search
- Bring up the words from the asset bank onto the Work area. Ask the children to highlight the 'ss' in each of the words, saying whether ss's position is at the beginning, the middle or the end of the word. Do not pronounce the words.

Reading
- Click the Reading tab for children to see the printed word. Note: Children *are not told* the word. The word is broken down into its constituent phonemes. Ask children to say each of the phonemes in the word.
- Click Blend to watch and hear the Bug's demonstration of how to blend the word.
- Click Undo and then ask a child to come to the Work area and move the arrow along. Encourage the whole class to blend the sounds out loud as the arrow moves along pushing the letters together. We recommend a smooth articulation of the sounds for blending.
- Work through each of the words in sequence. Click ▶ to change words.

Spelling
- The children return to their seats.
- Start by selecting the Words tab. Remember, the children do not see the word. Click Say to hear the word and ask the children to repeat it. Then ask the children to use their magnetic letters to make the word on their own magnetic boards, saying the word every time they look for a letter. Follow the procedure for word spelling on page 47.
- Ask a child to come up to the Work area to make the word. Did everyone get it right?
- Ask a child to use the arrow to push the letters together. Encourage the class to blend the word out loud.
- Repeat for the remaining word under the Words tab.
- Under the Pictures tab, click Show to display the image. You and the children say the picture word and proceed to spell it as before. Repeat if there is more than one image.

Writing
- Ask the children to find the letter 's' among their magnetic letters and to feel the shape of it. Click Show and ask the children to look and listen as the lowercase letters are formed.
- "Skywrite" the letters in the air, and ask the children to do the same as you say how to form the letters.
- Ask children to tell you how to write the letters as you write them on the empty Work area.
- Ask children to try to write the letters themselves using paper and pencil or individual whiteboard and pen.
- Select uppercase and repeat when you think this to be appropriate for your children.

WRAP-UP
- Recap the learning intentions with the children.
- Play the "This is 'ss'" video again, then play the alphabet song and encourage the children to sing along, signifying the end of the session.

Learning intentions are to:
- recap what we know
- say the /s/ phoneme
- find the letters 'ss'
- read words with 'ss' in
- spell words with 'ss' in
- write the letters 'ss'

Focus content: revision

Letters and Sounds
ck, e, u, r, h, b, f, ff, l, ll
Reading
let, tell, leg, doll
Writing and Spelling
h, b, f, ff, l, ll
lock, sell, dull, laptop

Focus content: lesson

Sounds
"This is 'ss'" video
Visual search
mess, lass, hiss, fuss
Reading
Audio: mess, lass, hiss, fuss
No audio: fusspot, loss, mass, toss
Spelling
Words tab: less, miss
Pictures tab: kiss, cross
Writing
ss

Next steps
- Play the online pupil games for Unit 4
- Complete the PCM for Unit 5 (ss)
- Read Phonics Bug books that practise ck, e, u, r:
  Get a Pet!
  In the Pit
  Is it a Rock?
  Sid and Duck
  Sid's Pet Rat
  Tut, Tut, Pup!

Unit 5

Language session

After: h, b, f, ff, l, ll, ss

INTRODUCTION
- Play the alphabet song twice, once with voice accompaniment, children listening and singing along with accompaniment, and once with children singing along to the music without voice accompaniment.
- Discuss with the children the learning intentions for the day.

IRREGULAR

Reading
- Click Show to display the words, and ask/teach the children how to read them. Click Answer to hear the correct pronunciation.
- Explain that 'I' (the capital letter) is also a word. Give examples, such as "I am a teacher", "I am happy".

Spelling
- Click Say to hear the word, and ask the children to repeat it.
- Put the word into a sentence, so that the children understand its meaning, for example, "I like chocolate", "She walked into the classroom".
- Ask the children to say the word ("I"), select the uppercase magnetic letter and drag the letter into the empty box.
- Ask the children to read the word.
- For the remaining word ("into"), ask the children to select the lowercase magnetic letters and drag each letter into its empty box. Ask the children to read the word.

LESSON

Reading
- Click Show to display the sentence, and ask the children to read it.
- Click Answer to see whether they are right.
- Repeat for the remaining sentences.

Spelling
- Click Say to hear the caption and ask the children to repeat it.
- Ask the children to help you to select the lowercase magnetic letters and drag the letters to the empty boxes on the Work area.
- Ask the children to read the caption.
- Repeat the procedure for the remaining captions.

Writing
- The children return to their seats.
- Click Say to hear the caption and ask the children to repeat it.
- Ask the children to tell you how to write the caption on the lines provided.
- Clear the screen. Ask the children to say the caption and try to write it using paper and pencil or individual whiteboard and pen.
- Click Answer to check whether they are right.
- Repeat for the remaining captions.

Follow-up
- Display the partial sentence with a picture taking the place of a missing word (bag). You and the children say the word.
- Ask the children to read the sentence, saying the picture word for the missing word. Spell the word using pencil and paper.
- Click on the picture itself to show the word. Ask the children to read it.

WRAP-UP
- Recap the learning intentions with the children.
- Play the alphabet song again and encourage the children to sing along, signifying the end of the session.

Learning intentions are to:
- learn to read and spell irregular words "I" and "into"
- learn to read and spell short captions

Focus content: irregular

Reading
I, into

Spelling
I, into

Focus content: lesson

Reading
Go into the hut.
Bill has a pet rat.
I pick it up.

Spelling
a mess, a hot pot, a big pig

Writing
a mess, a hot pot, a big pig

Follow-up
Picture shows: bag

Next steps
- Play the online pupil games for Unit 5
- Complete the language PCM for Unit 5
- Read Phonics Bug books that practise h, b, f, ff, l, ll, ss:
    - A Bad Lad
    - A Big Mess
    - Big Fat Rat
    - Doll is Ill
    - Huff! Puff!
    - The Bop

Unit 6

Target phoneme /j/ written as 'j'

INTRODUCTION
- Play the alphabet song twice, once with voice accompaniment, children listening and singing along with accompaniment, and once with children singing along to the music without voice accompaniment.
- Discuss with the children the learning intentions for the day.

REVISION
[previously taught grapheme–phoneme correspondences; blending phonemes for reading; segmenting spoken words for spelling]
- Go through the Revision screens at a brisk pace.
- Watch out for any children who have not remembered the phonemes or the graphemes.

LESSON
Sounds
- Choose the relevant lesson session.
- Play the "This is 'j'" video once through.
- Say the phoneme /j/, and ask the children to repeat it after you. Make sure you keep the sound pure and encourage the children to do the same.

Visual Search
- Bring up the words from the asset bank onto the Work area. Ask the children to highlight the 'j' in each of the words, saying whether j's position is at the beginning, the middle or the end of the word. Do not pronounce the words.

ⓘ The sound 'uh' (known as "schwa" and represented phonetically as /ə/) may be pronounced for the vowel in an unaccented or unstressed syllable – e.g. the 'a' in "alone" or the 'e' in "the". Any vowel can be pronounced in this way. As children will encounter many words containing the schwa sound, you may wish to highlight it as necessary.

Reading
- Click the Reading tab for children to see the printed word. Note: Children *are not told* the word. The word is broken down into its constituent phonemes. Ask children to say each of the phonemes in the word.
- Click Blend to watch and hear the Bug's demonstration of how to blend the word.
- Click Undo and then ask a child to come to the Work area and move the arrow along. Encourage the whole class to blend the sounds out loud as the arrow moves along pushing the letters together. We recommend a smooth articulation of the sounds for blending.
- Work through each of the words in sequence. Click ▶ to change words.

Spelling
- The children return to their seats.
- Start by selecting the Words tab. Remember, the children do not see the word. Click Say to hear the word and ask the children to repeat it. Then ask the children to use their magnetic letters to make the word on their own magnetic boards, saying the word every time they look for a letter. Follow the procedure for word spelling on page 47.
- Ask a child to come up to the Work area to make the word. Did everyone get it right?
- Ask a child to use the arrow to push the letters together. Encourage the class to blend the word out loud.
- Repeat for the remaining word under the Words tab.
- Under the Pictures tab, click Show to display the image. You and the children say the picture word and proceed to spell it as before. Repeat if there is more than one image.

Writing
- Ask the children to find the 'j' letter among their magnetic letters and to feel the shape of it. Click Show and ask the children to look and listen as the lowercase letter is formed.
- "Skywrite" the letter in the air, and ask the children to do the same as you say how to form the letter.
- Ask children to tell you how to write the letter as you write it on the empty Work area.
- Ask children to try to write the letter themselves using paper and pencil or individual whiteboard and pen.
- Select uppercase and repeat when you think this to be appropriate for your children.

WRAP-UP
- Recap the learning intentions with the children.
- Play the "This is 'j'" video again, then play the alphabet song and encourage the children to sing along, signifying the end of the session.

Learning intentions are to:
- recap what we know
- say the /j/ phoneme
- find the letter 'j'
- read words with 'j' in
- spell words with 'j' in
- write the letter 'j'

Focus content: revision

Letters and Sounds
e, u, r, h, b, f, ff, l, ll, ss
Reading
less, miss, cross, kiss
Writing and Spelling
b, f, ff, l, ll, ss
fuss, loss, mass, toss

Focus content: lesson

Sounds
"This is 'j'" video
Visual search
jot, job, inject, jackpot
Reading
Audio: jot, jab, jig, jackpot
No audio: Jill, jog, jut, jacket
Spelling
Words tab: Jim, jug
Pictures tab: jet, jam
Writing
j

Next steps
- Play the online pupil games for Unit 5
- Complete the phoneme PCM for Unit 6 (j)
- Read Phonics Bug books that practise h, b, f, ff, l, ll, ss:
    A Bad Lad
    A Big Mess
    Big Fat Rat
    Doll is Ill
    Huff! Puff!
    The Bop

Unit 6

Target phoneme /v/ written as 'v'

INTRODUCTION
- Play the alphabet song twice, once with voice accompaniment, children listening and singing along with accompaniment, and once with children singing along to the music without voice accompaniment.
- Discuss with the children the learning intentions for the day.

REVISION
[previously taught grapheme–phoneme correspondences; blending phonemes for reading; segmenting spoken words for spelling]
- Go through the Revision screens at a brisk pace.
- Watch out for any children who have not remembered the phonemes or the graphemes.

LESSON

Sounds
- Choose the relevant lesson session.
- Play the "This is 'v'" video once through.
- Say the phoneme /v/, and ask the children to repeat it after you. Make sure you keep the sound pure and encourage the children to do the same.

Visual Search
- Bring up the words from the asset bank onto the Work area. Ask the children to highlight the 'v' in each of the words, saying whether v's position is at the beginning, the middle or the end of the word. Do not pronounce the words.

Reading
- Click the Reading tab for children to see the printed word. Note: Children *are not told* the word. The word is broken down into its constituent phonemes. Ask children to say each of the phonemes in the word.
- Click Blend to watch and hear the Bug's demonstration of how to blend the word.
- Click Undo and then ask a child to come to the Work area and move the arrow along. Encourage the whole class to blend the sounds out loud as the arrow moves along pushing the letters together. We recommend a smooth articulation of the sounds for blending.
- Work through each of the words in sequence. Click ▶ to change words.

Note: Some 2-syllable words are included from this point. Rules for syllables are taught in Key Stage 1 (P2–3). We find, however, that children can cope with the 2-syllable words included in Reception (P1).

Spelling
- The children return to their seats.
- Start by selecting the Words tab. Remember, the children do not see the word. Click Say to hear the word and ask the children to repeat it. Then ask the children to use their magnetic letters to make the word on their own magnetic boards, saying the word every time they look for a letter. Follow the procedure for word spelling on page 47.
- Ask a child to come up to the Work area to make the word. Did everyone get it right?
- Ask a child to use the arrow to push the letters together. Encourage the class to blend the word out loud.
- Repeat for the remaining word under the Words tab.
- Under the Pictures tab, click Show to display the image. You and the children say the picture word and proceed to spell it as before. Repeat if there is more than one image.

Writing
- Ask the children to find the 'v' letter among their magnetic letters and to feel the shape of it. Click Show and ask the children to look and listen as the lowercase letter is formed.
- "Skywrite" the letter in the air, and ask the children to do the same as you say how to form the letter.
- Ask children to tell you how to write the letter as you write it on the empty Work area.
- Ask children to try to write the letter themselves using paper and pencil or individual whiteboard and pen.
- Select uppercase and repeat when you think this to be appropriate for your children.

WRAP-UP
- Recap the learning intentions with the children.
- Play the "This is 'v'" video again, then play the alphabet song and encourage the children to sing along, signifying the end of the session.

Learning intentions are to:
- recap what we know
- say the /v/ phoneme
- find the letter 'v'
- read words with 'v' in
- spell words with 'v' in
- write the letter 'v'

Focus content: revision

Letters and Sounds
u, r, h, b, f, ff, l, ll, ss, j
Reading
Jim, jug, jet, jam
Writing and Spelling
f, ff, l, ll, ss, j
Jill, jog, jut, jacket

Focus content: lesson

Sounds
"This is 'v'" video
Visual search
vat, velvet, vivid, visit
Reading
Audio: vat, vet, Kevin, visit
No audio: Viv, velvet, level, vivid
Spelling
Words tab: vim, Bev
Pictures tab: van, seven
Writing
v

Next steps
- Play the online pupil games for Unit 5
- Complete the phoneme PCM for Unit 6 (v)
- Read Phonics Bug books that practise h, b, f, ff, l, ll, ss:
  - A Bad Lad
  - A Big Mess
  - Big Fat Rat
  - Doll is Ill
  - Huff! Puff!
  - The Bop

Unit 6

Target phoneme /w/ written as 'w'

INTRODUCTION
- Play the alphabet song twice, once with voice accompaniment, children listening and singing along with accompaniment, and once with children singing along to the music without voice accompaniment.
- Discuss with the children the learning intentions for the day.

REVISION
[previously taught grapheme–phoneme correspondences; blending phonemes for reading; segmenting spoken words for spelling]
- Go through the Revision screens at a brisk pace.
- Watch out for any children who have not remembered the phonemes or the graphemes.

LESSON

Sounds
- Choose the relevant lesson session.
- Play the "This is 'w'" video once through.
- Say the phoneme /w/, and ask the children to repeat it after you. Make sure you keep the sound pure and encourage the children to do the same.

Visual Search
- Bring up the words from the asset bank onto the Work area. Ask the children to highlight the 'w' in each of the words, saying whether w's position is at the beginning, the middle or the end of the word. Do not pronounce the words.

Reading
- Click the Reading tab for children to see the printed word. Note: Children *are not told* the word. The word is broken down into its constituent phonemes. Ask children to say each of the phonemes in the word.
- Click Blend to watch and hear the Bug's demonstration of how to blend the word.
- Click Undo and then ask a child to come to the Work area and move the arrow along. Encourage the whole class to blend the sounds out loud as the arrow moves along, pushing the letters together. We recommend a smooth articulation of the sounds for blending.
- Work through each of the words in sequence. Click ▶ to change words.

Spelling
- The children return to their seats.
- Start by selecting the Words tab. Remember, the children do not see the word. Click Say to hear the word and ask the children to repeat it. Then ask the children to use their magnetic letters to make the word on their own magnetic boards, saying the word every time they look for a letter. Follow the procedure for word spelling on page 47.
- Ask a child to come up to the Work area to make the word. Did everyone get it right?
- Ask a child to use the arrow to push the letters together. Encourage the class to blend the word out loud.
- Repeat for the remaining word under the Words tab.
- Under the Pictures tab, click Show to display the image. You and the children say the picture word and proceed to spell it as before. Repeat if there is more than one image.

Writing
- Ask the children to find the 'w' letter among their magnetic letters and to feel the shape of it. Click Show and ask the children to look and listen as the lowercase letter is formed.
- "Skywrite" the letter in the air, and ask the children to do the same as you say how to form the letter.
- Ask children to tell you how to write the letter as you write it on the empty Work area.
- Ask children to try to write the letter themselves using paper and pencil or individual whiteboard and pen.
- Select uppercase and repeat when you think this to be appropriate for your children.

WRAP-UP
- Recap the learning intentions with the children.
- Play the "This is 'w'" video again, then play the alphabet song and encourage the children to sing along, signifying the end of the session.

Learning intentions are to:
- recap what we know
- say the /w/ phoneme
- find the letter 'w'
- read words with 'w' in
- spell words with 'w' in
- write the letter 'w'

Focus content: revision

Letters and Sounds
r, h, b, f, ff, l, ll, ss, j, v
Reading
vim, Bev, van, seven
Writing and Spelling
l, ll, ss, j, v
Viv, velvet, level, vivid

Focus content: lesson

Sounds
"This is 'w'" video
Visual search
swim, west, wagon, wigwam
Reading
Audio: wag, wet, wit, wigwam
No audio: web, will, twig, wagon
Spelling
Words tab: win, wick
Pictures tab: swim, wigwam
Writing
w

Next steps
- Play the online pupil games for Unit 5
- Complete the phoneme PCM for Unit 6 (w)
- Read Phonics Bug books that practise h, b, f, ff, l, ll, ss:
    A Bad Lad
    A Big Mess
    Big Fat Rat
    Doll is Ill
    Huff! Puff!
    The Bop

Unit 6

Target phoneme /x/ written as 'x'

INTRODUCTION
- Play the alphabet song twice, once with voice accompaniment, children listening and singing along with accompaniment, and once with children singing along to the music without voice accompaniment.
- Discuss with the children the learning intentions for the day.

REVISION
[previously taught grapheme–phoneme correspondences; blending phonemes for reading; segmenting spoken words for spelling]
- Go through the Revision screens at a brisk pace.
- Watch out for any children who have not remembered the phonemes or the graphemes.

LESSON

Sounds
- Choose the relevant lesson session.
- Play the "This is 'x'" video once through.
- Say the phoneme /x/ (x = /ks/), and ask the children to repeat it after you. Make sure you keep the sound pure and encourage the children to do the same.

Visual Search
- Bring up the words from the asset bank onto the Work area. Ask the children to highlight the 'x' in each of the words, saying whether x's position is at the beginning, the middle or the end of the word. Do not pronounce the words.

Reading
- Click the Reading tab for children to see the printed word. Note: Children *are not told* the word. The word is broken down into its constituent phonemes. Ask children to say each of the phonemes in the word.
- Click Blend to watch and hear the Bug's demonstration of how to blend the word.
- Click Undo and then ask a child to come to the Work area and move the arrow along. Encourage the whole class to blend the sounds out loud as the arrow moves along pushing the letters together. We recommend a smooth articulation of the sounds for blending.
- Work through each of the words in sequence. Click ▶ to change words.

Spelling
- The children return to their seats.
- Start by selecting the Words tab. Remember, the children do not see the word. Click Say to hear the word and ask the children to repeat it. Then ask the children to use their magnetic letters to make the word on their own magnetic boards, saying the word every time they look for a letter. Follow the procedure for word spelling on page 47.
- Ask a child to come up to the Work area to make the word. Did everyone get it right?
- Ask a child to use the arrow to push the letters together. Encourage the class to blend the word out loud.
- Repeat for the remaining word under the Words tab.
- Under the Pictures tab, click Show to display the image. You and the children say the picture word and proceed to spell it as before. Repeat if there is more than one image.

Writing
- Ask the children to find the 'x' letter among their magnetic letters and to feel the shape of it. Click Show and ask children to look and listen as the lowercase letter is formed.
- "Skywrite" the letter in the air, and ask the children to do the same as you say how to form the letter.
- Ask children to tell you how to write the letter as you write it on the empty Work area.
- Ask children to try to write the letter themselves using paper and pencil or individual whiteboard and pen.
- Select uppercase and repeat when you think this to be appropriate for your children.

WRAP-UP
- Recap the learning intentions with the children.
- Play the "This is 'x'" video again, then play the alphabet song and encourage the children to sing along, signifying the end of the session.

Learning intentions are to:
- recap what we know
- say the /x/ phoneme
- find the letter 'x'
- read words with 'x' in
- spell words with 'x' in
- write the letter 'x'

Focus content: revision

Letters and Sounds
h, b, f, ff, l, ll, ss, j, v, w
Reading
win, wick, swim, wigwam
Writing and Spelling
ss, j, v, w
web, will, twig, wagon

Focus content: lesson

Sounds
"This is 'x'" video
Visual search
exit, box, fox, mix
Reading
Audio: box, Max, exit, taxi
No audio: mix, flex, tax, vixen
Spelling
Words tab: fix, wax
Pictures tab: fox, six
Writing
x

Next steps
- Play the online pupil games for Unit 5
- Complete the phoneme PCM for Unit 6 (x)
- Read Phonics Bug books that practise h, b, f, ff, l, ll, ss:
  - A Bad Lad
  - A Big Mess
  - Big Fat Rat
  - Doll is Ill
  - Huff! Puff!
  - The Bop

Unit 6

Language session

After: j, v, w, x

INTRODUCTION
- Play the alphabet song twice, once with voice accompaniment, children listening and singing along with accompaniment, and once with children singing along to the music without voice accompaniment.
- Discuss with the children the learning intentions for the day.

IRREGULAR

Reading
- Click Show to display the words, and ask/teach the children how to read them. Click Answer to hear the correct pronunciation.
- Explain that in the words "me" and "be", 'e' sounds like its letter name, pronounced /ee/.

Spelling
- Click Say to hear the word, and ask the children to repeat it.
- Put the word into a sentence, so that the children understand its meaning, for example, "He gave me a notebook", "In January I will be five".
- Ask the children to say the word, help to select the lowercase magnetic letters and drag each letter into its empty box.
- Ask the children to read the word.
- Repeat for the remaining word.

LESSON

Reading
- Click Show to display the sentence, and ask the children to read it.
- Click Answer to reveal whether they are right.
- Repeat for the remaining sentences. Note that one sentence is a question.

Spelling
- Click Say to hear the caption and ask the children to repeat it.
- Ask the children to help you to select the lowercase magnetic letters and drag the letters to the empty boxes on the Work area.
- Ask the children to read the caption.
- Repeat the procedure for the remaining captions.

Writing
- The children return to their seats.
- Click Say to hear the caption and ask the children to repeat it.
- Ask the children to tell you how to write the caption on the lines provided.
- Clear the screen. Ask the children to say the caption and try to write it using paper and pencil or individual whiteboard and pen.
- Click Answer to check whether they are right.
- Repeat for the remaining captions.

Follow-up
- Display the partial sentence with a picture taking the place of a missing word (duck). You and the children say the word.
- Ask the children to read the sentence, saying the picture word for the missing word. Spell the word, using paper and pencil.
- Click on the picture itself to show the word.

WRAP-UP
- Recap the learning intentions with the children.
- Play the alphabet song again and encourage the children to sing along, signifying the end of the session.

Learning intentions are to:
- learn to read and spell the irregular words "me" and "be"
- learn to read and spell short captions

Focus content: irregular

Reading
me, be

Spelling
me, be

Focus content: lesson

Reading
Get me a taxi.
Will a fox win a jackpot?
No, it will not.

Spelling
a pot of jam, a wet wig, jig and jog

Writing
a pot of jam, a wet wig, jig and jog

Follow-up
Picture shows: duck

Next steps
- Play the online language pupil games for Unit 6
- Complete the language PCM for Unit 6
- Read Phonics Bug books that practise j, v, w, x:
    A Big Win
    Go To Bed
    I Can Fix It!
    Jack Gets a Pet
    Max's Box
    Nan's Man
    Sid is Sick
    Stan and Vick
    The Van

Unit 7

Target phoneme /y/ written as 'y'

INTRODUCTION
- Play the alphabet song twice, once with voice accompaniment, children listening and singing along with accompaniment, and once with children singing along to the music without voice accompaniment.
- Discuss with the children the learning intentions for the day.

REVISION
[previously taught grapheme–phoneme correspondences; blending phonemes for reading; segmenting spoken words for spelling]
- Go through the Revision screens at a brisk pace.
- Remind the children about the concept of two letters making one sound, e.g. 'ff' in "off".
- Watch out for any children who have not remembered the phonemes or the graphemes.

LESSON

Sounds
- Choose the relevant lesson session.
- Play the "This is 'y'" video once through.
- Say the phoneme /y/, and ask the children to repeat it after you. Make sure you keep the sound pure and encourage the children to do the same.

Visual Search
- Bring up the words from the asset bank onto the Work area. Ask the children to highlight the 'y' in each of the words, saying whether y's position is at the beginning, the middle or the end of the word. Do not pronounce the words.

Reading
- Click the Reading tab for children to see the printed word. Note: Children *are not told* the word. The word is broken down into its constituent phonemes. Ask children to say each of the phonemes in the word.
- Click Blend to watch and hear the Bug's demonstration of how to blend the word.
- Click Undo and then ask a child to come to the Work area and move the arrow along. Encourage the whole class to blend the sounds out loud as the arrow moves along pushing the letters together. We recommend a smooth articulation of the sounds for blending.
- Work through each of the words in sequence. Click ▶ to change words.

Spelling
- The children return to their seats.
- Start by selecting the Words tab. Remember, the children do not see the word. Click Say to hear the word and ask the children to repeat it. Then ask the children to use their magnetic letters to make the word on their own magnetic boards, saying the word every time they look for a letter. Follow the procedure for word spelling on page 47.
- Ask a child to come up to the Work area to make the word. Did everyone get it right?
- Ask a child to use the arrow to push the letters together. Encourage the class to blend the word out loud.
- Repeat for the remaining word under the Words tab.
- Under the Pictures tab, click Show to display the image. You and the children say the picture word and proceed to spell it as before. Repeat if there is more than one image.

Writing
- Ask the children to find the 'y' letter among their magnetic letters and to feel the shape of it. Click Show and ask the children to look and listen as the lowercase letter is formed.
- "Skywrite" the letter in the air, and ask the children to do the same as you say how to form the letter.
- Ask children to tell you how to write the letter as you write it on the empty Work area.
- Ask children to try to write the letter themselves using paper and pencil or individual whiteboard and pen.
- Select uppercase and repeat when you think this to be appropriate for your children.

WRAP-UP
- Recap the learning intentions with the children.
- Play the "This is 'y'" video again, then play the alphabet song and encourage the children to sing along, signifying the end of the session.

Learning intentions are to:
- recap what we know
- say the phoneme /y/
- find the letter 'y'
- read words with 'y' in
- spell words with 'y' in
- write the letter 'y'

Focus content: revision

Letters and Sounds
b, f, ff, l, ll, ss, j, v, w, x
Reading
fix, wax, fox, six
Writing and Spelling
j, v, w, x
mix, flex, tax, vixen

Focus content: lesson

Sounds
"This is 'y'" video
Visual search
yet, yak, yam, yelp
Reading
Audio: yet, yes, yak, yell
No audio: yam, yen, yelp, canyon
Spelling
Words tab: yes, yap
Pictures tab: yell, yak
Writing
y

Next steps
- Play the online pupil games for Unit 6
- Complete the phoneme PCM for Unit 7 (y)
- Read Phonics Bug books that practise j, v, w, x:
  - A Big Win
  - Go To Bed
  - I Can Fix It!
  - Jack Gets a Pet
  - Max's Box
  - Nan's Man
  - Sid is Sick
  - Stan and Vick
  - The Van

Unit 7

Target phoneme /z/ written as 'z' and 'zz'

INTRODUCTION
- Play the alphabet song twice, once with voice accompaniment, children listening and singing along with accompaniment, and once with children singing along to the music without voice accompaniment.
- Discuss with the children the learning intentions for the day.

REVISION
[previously taught grapheme–phoneme correspondences; blending phonemes for reading; segmenting spoken words for spelling]
- Go through the Revision screens at a brisk pace.
- Watch out for any children who have not remembered the phonemes or the graphemes.

LESSON

Sounds
- Choose the relevant lesson session.
- Remind the children about the concept of two letters making one sound, e.g. 'ff' in "off".
- Play the "This is 'z'" video once through.
- Say the phoneme /z/, and ask the children to repeat it after you. Make sure you keep the sound pure and encourage the children to do the same.

Visual Search
- Bring up the words from the asset bank onto the Work area. Ask the children to highlight the 'z' or 'zz' in each of the words, saying whether the position of z or zz is at the beginning, the middle or the end of the word. Do not pronounce the words.

Reading
- Click the Reading tab for children to see the printed word. Note: Children *are not told* the word. The word is broken down into its constituent phonemes. Ask children to say each of the phonemes in the word.
- Click Blend to watch and hear the Bug's demonstration of how to blend the word.
- Click Undo and then ask a child to come to the Work area and move the arrow along. Encourage the whole class to blend the sounds out loud as the arrow moves along pushing the letters together. We recommend a smooth articulation of the sounds for blending.
- Work through each of the words in sequence. Click ▶ to change words.

Spelling
- The children return to their seats.
- Start by selecting the Words tab. Remember, the children do not see the word. Click Say to hear the word and ask the children to repeat it. Then ask the children to use their magnetic letters to make the word on their own magnetic boards, saying the word every time they look for a letter. Follow the procedure for word spelling on page 47.
- Ask a child to come up to the Work area to make the word. Did everyone get it right?
- Ask a child to use the arrow to push the letters together. Encourage the class to blend the word out loud.
- Repeat for the remaining word under the Words tab.
- Under the Pictures tab, click Show to display the image. You and the children say the picture word and proceed to spell it as before. Repeat if there is more than one image.

Writing
- Ask the children to find the 'z' letter among their magnetic letters and to feel the shape of it. Click Show and ask the children to look and listen as the lowercase letter is formed.
- "Skywrite" the letter(s) in the air, and ask the children to do the same as you say how to form the letter.
- Ask children to tell you how to write the letter(s) as you write it (them) on the empty Work area.
- Ask children to try to write the letter(s) themselves using paper and pencil or individual whiteboard and pen.
- Select uppercase and repeat when you think this to be appropriate for your children.

WRAP-UP
- Recap the learning intentions with the children.
- Play the "This is 'z'" video again, then play the alphabet song and encourage the children to sing along, signifying the end of the session.

Learning intentions are to:
- recap what we know
- say the phoneme /z/
- find the letters 'z' and 'zz'
- read words with 'z' or 'zz' in
- spell words with 'z' or 'zz' in
- write the letter 'z'

Focus content: revision

Letters and Sounds
f, ff, l, ll, ss, j, v, w, x, y
Reading
yes, yap, yell, yak
Writing and Spelling
v, w, x, y
yam, yen, yelp, yum

Focus content: lesson

Sounds
"This is 'z'" video
Visual search
jazz, zebra, zigzag, fuzz
Reading
Audio: zap, zest, buzz, fizz
No audio: fez, jazz, fuzz, zigzag
Spelling
Words tab: zed, Zak
Pictures tab: zip, zebra
Writing
z, zz

Next steps
- Play the online pupil games for Unit 6
- Complete the phoneme PCM for Unit 7 (z)
- Read Phonics Bug books that practise j, v, w, x:
  - A Big Win
  - Go To Bed
  - I Can Fix It!
  - Jack Gets a Pet
  - Max's Box
  - Nan's Man
  - Sid is Sick
  - Stan and Vick
  - The Van

Unit 7

Target phoneme /qu/ written as 'qu'

INTRODUCTION
- Play the alphabet song twice, once with voice accompaniment, children listening and singing along with accompaniment, and once with children singing along to the music without voice accompaniment.
- Discuss with the children the learning intentions for the day.

REVISION
[previously taught grapheme–phoneme correspondences; blending phonemes for reading; segmenting spoken words for spelling]
- Go through the Revision screens at a brisk pace.
- Watch out for any children who have not remembered the phonemes or the graphemes.

LESSON

Sounds
- Choose the relevant lesson session.
- Play the "This is 'qu'" video once through.
- Say the phoneme /qu/ (actually two phonemes: qu = /cw/), and ask the children to repeat it after you. Make sure you keep the sound pure and encourage the children to do the same.

Visual Search
- Bring up the words from the asset bank onto the Work area. Ask the children to highlight the 'qu' in each of the words, saying whether qu's position is at the beginning, the middle or the end of the word. Do not pronounce the words.

Reading
- Click the Reading tab for children to see the printed word. Note: Children *are not told* the word. The word is broken down into its constituent phonemes. Ask children to say each of the phonemes in the word.
- Click Blend to watch and hear the Bug's demonstration of how to blend the word.
- Click Undo and then ask a child to come to the Work area and move the arrow along. Encourage the whole class to blend the sounds out loud as the arrow moves along pushing the letters together. We recommend a smooth articulation of the sounds for blending.
- Work through each of the words in sequence. Click ▶ to change words.

Spelling
- The children return to their seats.
- Start by selecting the Words tab. Remember, the children do not see the word. Click Say to hear the word and ask the children to repeat it. Then ask the children to use their magnetic letters to make the word on their own magnetic boards, saying the word every time they look for a letter. Follow the procedure for word spelling on page 47.
- Ask a child to come up to the Work area to make the word. Did everyone get it right?
- Ask a child to use the arrow to push the letters together. Encourage the class to blend the word out loud.
- Repeat for the remaining word under the Words tab.
- Under the Pictures tab, click Show to display the image. You and the children say the picture word and proceed to spell it as before. Repeat if there is more than one image.

Writing
- Ask the children to find the letters 'q' and 'u' among their magnetic letters and to feel the shape of them. Click Show and ask the children to look and listen as the lowercase letters are formed.
- "Skywrite" the letters in the air, and ask the children to do the same as you say how to form the letters.
- Ask children to tell you how to write the letters as you write them on the empty Work area.
- Ask children to try to write the letters themselves using paper and pencil or individual whiteboard and pen.
- Select uppercase and repeat when you think this to be appropriate for your children.

WRAP-UP
- Recap the learning intentions with the children.
- Play the "This is 'qu'" video again, then play the alphabet song and encourage the children to sing along, signifying the end of the session.

Learning intentions are to:
- recap what we know
- say the phoneme /qu/
- find the letters 'qu'
- read words with 'qu' in
- spell words with 'qu' in
- write the letters 'qu'

Focus content: revision

Letters and Sounds
l, ll, ss, j, v, w, x, y, z, zz
Reading
zed, Zak, zip, zebra
Writing and Spelling
w, x, y, z, zz
fez, jazz, fuzz, zigzag

Focus content: lesson

Sounds
"This is 'qu'" video
Visual search
quack, quilt, squid, squint
Reading
Audio: quit, quip, quick, squid
No audio: quid, liquid, quicken, quiff
Spelling
Words tab: quiz, quack
Pictures tab: quilt, quill
Writing
qu

Next steps
- Play the online pupil games for Unit 6
- Complete the phoneme PCM for Unit 7 (qu)
- Read Phonics Bug books that practise j, v, w, x:
    - A Big Win
    - Go To Bed
    - I Can Fix It!
    - Jack Gets a Pet
    - Max's Box
    - Nan's Man
    - Sid is Sick
    - Stan and Vick
    - The Van

Language session

After: y, z, zz, qu

INTRODUCTION
- Play the alphabet song twice, once with voice accompaniment, children listening and singing along with accompaniment, and once with children singing along to the music without voice accompaniment.
- Discuss with the children the learning intentions for the day.

IRREGULAR

Reading
- Click Show to display the words, and ask/teach the children how to read them. Click Answer to hear the correct pronunciation.
- Explain that 'y' is sometimes used as a vowel instead of 'i', pronounced /ie/. In the word "he", 'e' sounds like its letter name, pronounced /ee/.

Spelling
- Click Say to hear the word, and ask the children to repeat it.
- Put the word into a sentence, so that the children understand its meaning, for example, "He is tall", "This is my cat", "This is a painting by Jim".
- Ask the children to say the word, help to select the lowercase magnetic letters and drag each letter into its empty box.
- Ask the children to read the word.
- Repeat for the remaining words.

LESSON

Reading
- Click Show to display the sentence, and ask the children to read it.
- Click Answer to reveal whether they are right.
- Repeat for the remaining sentences. Note that one sentence is a question.

Spelling
- Click Say to hear the caption and ask the children to repeat it.
- Ask the children to help you to select the lowercase magnetic letters and drag the letters to the empty boxes on the Work area.
- Ask the children to read the caption.
- Repeat the procedure for the remaining captions.

Writing
- The children return to their seats.
- Click Say to hear the caption and ask the children to repeat it.
- Ask the children to tell you how to write the caption on the lines provided.
- Clear the screen. Ask the children to say the caption and try to write it using paper and pencil or individual whiteboard and pen.
- Click Answer to check whether they are right.
- Repeat for the remaining captions.

Follow-up
- Display the partial sentence with a picture taking the place of a missing word (dog). You and the children say the word.
- Ask the children to read the sentence, saying the picture word for the missing word. Spell the word, using paper and pencil.
- Click on the picture itself to show the word.

WRAP-UP
- Recap the learning intentions with the children.
- Play the alphabet song again and encourage the children to sing along, signifying the end of the session.

Unit 7

Learning intentions are to:
- learn to read and spell the irregular words "he", "my" and "by"
- learn to read and spell short captions

Focus content: irregular

Reading
he, my, by

Spelling
he, my, by

Focus content: lesson

Reading
I can pack my quill pen in a box. Will Jack win the quiz? Yes, he will win it.

Spelling
not yet, yes and no, quick as a fox

Writing
not yet, yes and no, quick as a fox

Follow-up
Picture shows: dog

Next steps
- Play the online pupil games for Unit 7
- Complete the language PCM for Unit 7
- Read Phonics Bug books that practise y, z, zz qu:
  - A Picnic
  - Is It Quick?
  - Quick! Quick! Quick!
  - Quick Quiz
  - Sid and Zak
  - Slip, Slap, Slop!
  - The Fox and the Ducks
  - The Hunt
  - Zap!

Unit 8

Target phoneme /ch/ written as 'ch'

INTRODUCTION
- Play the alphabet song twice, once with voice accompaniment, children listening and singing along with accompaniment, and once with children singing along to the music without voice accompaniment.
- Discuss with the children the learning intentions for the day.

REVISION
[previously taught grapheme–phoneme correspondences; blending phonemes for reading; segmenting spoken words for spelling]
- Go through the Revision screens at a brisk pace.
- Remind the children about the concept of two letters making one sound, e.g. 'ff' in "off".
- Watch out for any children who have not remembered the phonemes or the graphemes.

LESSON
Sounds
- Choose the relevant lesson session.
- Play the "This is 'ch'" video once through.
- Say the phoneme /ch/ and ask the children to repeat it after you. Make sure you keep the sound pure and encourage the children to do the same.

Visual Search
- Bring up the words from the asset bank onto the Work area. Ask the children to highlight the 'ch' in each of the words, saying whether ch's position is at the beginning, the middle or the end of the word. Do not pronounce the words.

Reading
- Click the Reading tab for children to see the printed word. Note: Children *are not told* the word. The word is broken down into its constituent phonemes. Ask children to say each of the phonemes in the word.
- Click Blend to watch and hear the Bug's demonstration of how to blend the word.
- Click Undo and then ask a child to come to the Work area and move the arrow along. Encourage the whole class to blend the sounds out loud as the arrow moves along pushing the letters together. We recommend a smooth articulation of the sounds for blending.
- Work through each of the words in sequence. Click ▶ to change words.

Spelling
- The children return to their seats.
- Start by selecting the Words tab. Remember, the children do not see the word. Click Say to hear the word and ask the children to repeat it. Then ask the children to use their magnetic letters to make the word on their own magnetic boards, saying the word every time they look for a letter. Follow the procedure for word spelling on page 47.
- Ask a child to come up to the Work area to make the word. Did everyone get it right?
- Ask a child to use the arrow to push the letters together. Encourage the class to blend the word out loud.
- Repeat for the remaining word under the Words tab.
- Under the Pictures tab, click Show to display the image. You and the children say the picture word and proceed to spell it as before. Repeat if there is more than one image.

Writing
- Ask the children to find the letters 'c' and 'h' among their magnetic letters and to feel the shape of them. Click Show and ask the children to look and listen as the lowercase letters are formed.
- "Skywrite" the letters in the air, and ask the children to do the same as you say how to form the letters.
- Ask children to tell you how to write the letters as you write them on the empty Work area.
- Ask children to try to write the letters themselves using paper and pencil or individual whiteboard and pen.
- Select uppercase and repeat when you think this to be appropriate for your children.

WRAP-UP
- Recap the learning intentions with the children.
- Play the "This is 'ch'" video again, then play the alphabet song and encourage the children to sing along, signifying the end of the session.

Learning intentions are to:
- recap what we know
- say the phoneme /ch/
- find the letters 'ch'
- read words with 'ch' in
- spell words with 'ch' in
- write the letters 'ch'

Focus content: revision

Letters and Sounds
ss, j, v, w, x, y, z, zz, qu
Reading
quiz, quack, squid, quill
Writing and Spelling
x, y, z, zz, qu
quid, liquid, quicken, quiff

Focus content: lesson

Sounds
"This is 'ch'" video
Visual search
chum, much, chop, lunches
Reading
Audio: chum, much, chop, chug
No audio: check, such, chill, chicken
Spelling
Words tab: chat, chin
Pictures tab: chest, chips
Writing
ch

Next steps
- Play the online pupil games for Unit 7
- Complete the phoneme PCM for Unit 8 (ch)
- Read Phonics Bug books that practise y, z, zz, qu:
  A Picnic
  Is It Quick?
  Quick! Quick! Quick!
  Quick Quiz
  Sid and Zak
  Slip, Slap, Slop!
  The Fox and the Ducks
  The Hunt
  Zap!

Unit 8

Target phoneme /sh/ written as 'sh'

INTRODUCTION
- Play the alphabet song twice, once with voice accompaniment, children listening and singing along with accompaniment, and once with children singing along to the music without voice accompaniment.
- Discuss with the children the learning intentions for the day.

REVISION
[previously taught grapheme–phoneme correspondences; blending phonemes for reading; segmenting spoken words for spelling]
- Go through the Revision screens at a brisk pace.
- Watch out for any children who have not remembered the phonemes or the graphemes.

LESSON

Sounds
- Choose the relevant lesson session.
- Play the "This is 'sh'" video once through.
- Say the phoneme /sh/, and ask the children to repeat it after you. Make sure you keep the sound pure and encourage the children to do the same.

Visual Search
- Bring up the words from the asset bank onto the Work area. Ask the children to highlight the 'sh' in each of the words, saying whether sh's position is at the beginning, the middle or the end of the word. Do not pronounce the words.

Reading
- Click the Reading tab for children to see the printed word. Note: Children *are not told* the word. The word is broken down into its constituent phonemes. Ask children to say each of the phonemes in the word.
- Click Blend to watch and hear the Bug's demonstration of how to blend the word.
- Click Undo and then ask a child to come to the Work area and move the arrow along. Encourage the whole class to blend the sounds out loud as the arrow moves along pushing the letters together. We recommend a smooth articulation of the sounds for blending.
- Work through each of the words in sequence. Click ▶ to change words.

Spelling
- The children return to their seats.
- Start by selecting the Words tab. Remember, the children do not see the word. Click Say to hear the word and ask the children to repeat it. Then ask the children to use their magnetic letters to make the word on their own magnetic boards, saying the word every time they look for a letter. Follow the procedure for word spelling on page 47.
- Ask a child to come up to the Work area to make the word. Did everyone get it right?
- Ask a child to use the arrow to push the letters together. Encourage the class to blend the word out loud.
- Repeat for the remaining word under the Words tab.
- Under the Pictures tab, click Show to display the image. You and the children say the picture word and proceed to spell it as before. Repeat if there is more than one image.

Writing
- Ask the children to find the letters 's' and 'h' among their magnetic letters and to feel the shape of them. Click Show and ask the children to look and listen as the lowercase letters are formed.
- "Skywrite" the letters in the air, and ask the children to do the same as you say how to form the letters.
- Ask children to tell you how to write the letters as you write them on the empty Work area.
- Ask children to try to write the letters themselves using paper and pencil or individual whiteboard and pen.
- Select uppercase and repeat when you think this to be appropriate for your children.

WRAP-UP
- Recap the learning intentions with the children.
- Play the "This is 'sh'" video again, then play the alphabet song and encourage the children to sing along, signifying the end of the session.

Learning intentions are to:
- recap what we know
- say the phoneme /sh/
- find the letters 'sh'
- read words with 'sh' in
- spell words with 'sh' in
- write the letters 'sh'

Focus content: revision

Letters and Sounds
j, v, w, x, y, z, zz, qu, ch
Reading
chat, chin, chest, chips
Writing and Spelling
y, z, zz, qu, ch
check, such, chill, chicken

Focus content: lesson

Sounds
"This is 'sh'" video
Visual search
fish, shut, dishes, Josh
Reading
Audio: shut, dish, Josh, shock
No audio: shop, cash, rush, shed
Spelling
Words tab: ship, flash
Pictures tab: fish, shell
Writing
sh

Next steps
- Play the online pupil games for Unit 7
- Complete the phoneme PCM for Unit 8 (sh)
- Read Phonics Bug books that practise y, z, zz, qu:
  A Picnic
  Is It Quick?
  Quick! Quick! Quick!
  Quick Quiz
  Sid and Zak
  Slip, Slap, Slop!
  The Fox and the Ducks
  The Hunt
  Zap!

Unit 8

Target phoneme /th/ written as 'th'

INTRODUCTION
- Play the alphabet song twice, once with voice accompaniment, children listening and singing along with accompaniment, and once with children singing along to the music without voice accompaniment.
- Discuss with the children the learning intentions for the day.

REVISION
(previously taught grapheme–phoneme correspondences; blending phonemes for reading; segmenting spoken words for spelling)
- Go through the Revision screens at a brisk pace.
- Watch out for any children who have not remembered the phonemes or the graphemes.

LESSON

Sounds
- Choose the relevant lesson session.
- Play the "This is 'th'" video once through. If appropriate, explain that 'th' sounds slightly differently in some words – 'th' in "with" has a buzzing sound, whereas 'th' in "thin" does not.
- Say the phoneme 'th', and ask the children to repeat it after you. Make sure you keep the sound pure and encourage the children to do the same.

Visual Search
- Bring up the words from the asset bank onto the Work area. Ask the children to highlight the 'th' in each of the words, saying whether th's position is at the beginning, the middle or the end of the word. Do not pronounce the words.

Reading
- Click the Reading tab for children to see the printed word. Note: Children *are not told* the word. The word is broken down into its constituent phonemes. Ask children to say each of the phonemes in the word.
- Click Blend to watch and hear the Bug's demonstration of how to blend the word.
- Click Undo and then ask a child to come to the Work area and move the arrow along. Encourage the whole class to blend the sounds out loud as the arrow moves along pushing the letters together. We recommend a smooth articulation of the sounds for blending.
- Work through each of the words in sequence. Click ▶ to change words.

Spelling
- The children return to their seats.
- Start by selecting the Words tab. Remember, the children do not see the word. Click Say to hear the word and ask the children to repeat it. Then ask the children to use their magnetic letters to make the word on their own magnetic boards, saying the word every time they look for a letter. Follow the procedure for word spelling on page 47.
- Ask a child to come up to the Work area to make the word. Did everyone get it right?
- Ask a child to use the arrow to push the letters together. Encourage the class to blend the word out loud.
- Repeat for the remaining word under the Words tab.
- Under the Pictures tab, click Show to display the image. You and the children say the picture word and proceed to spell it as before. Repeat if there is more than one image.

Writing
- Ask the children to find the letters 't' and 'h' among their magnetic letters and to feel the shape of them. Click Show and ask the children to look and listen as the lowercase letters are formed.
- "Skywrite" the letters in the air, and ask the children to do the same as you say how to form the letters.
- Ask children to tell you how to write the letters as you write them on the empty Work area.
- Ask children to try to write the letters themselves using paper and pencil or individual whiteboard and pen.
- Select uppercase and repeat when you think this to be appropriate for your children.

WRAP-UP
- Recap the learning intentions with the children.
- Play the "This is 'th'" video again, then play the alphabet song and encourage the children to sing along, signifying the end of the session.

Learning intentions are to:
- recap what we know
- say the phoneme /th/
- find the letters 'th'
- read words with 'th' in
- spell words with 'th' in
- write the letters 'th'

Focus content: revision

Letters and Sounds
v, w, x, y, z, zz, qu, ch, sh
Reading
ship, flash, fish, shell
Writing and Spelling
z, zz, qu, ch, sh
shop, cash, rush, shed

Focus content: lesson

Sounds
"This is 'th'" video
Visual search
maths, cloth, thin, Beth
Reading
Audio: thud, Beth, them, cloth
No audio: that, then, thick, froth
Spelling
Words tab: with, this
Pictures tab: moth, thin
Writing
th

Next steps
- Play the online pupil games for Unit 7
- Complete the phoneme PCM for Unit 8 (th)
- Read Phonics Bug books that practise y, z, zz, qu:
  A Picnic
  Is It Quick?
  Quick! Quick! Quick!
  Quick Quiz
  Sid and Zak
  Slip, Slap, Slop!
  The Fox and the Ducks
  The Hunt
  Zap!

Unit 8

Target phoneme /ng/ written as 'ng'

INTRODUCTION
- Play the alphabet song twice, once with voice accompaniment, children listening and singing along with accompaniment, and once with the children singing along to the music without voice accompaniment.
- Discuss with the children the learning intentions for the day.

REVISION
[previously taught grapheme–phoneme correspondences; blending phonemes for reading; segmenting spoken words for spelling]
- Go through the Revision screens at a brisk pace.
- Watch out for any children who have not remembered the phonemes or the graphemes.

LESSON

Sounds
- Choose the relevant lesson session.
- Play the "This is 'ng'" video once through.
- Say the phoneme /ng/, and ask the children to repeat it after you. Make sure you keep the sound pure and encourage the children to do the same.

Visual Search
- Bring up the words from the asset bank onto the Work area. Ask the children to highlight the 'ng' in each of the words, saying whether ng's position is at the beginning, the middle or the end of the word. Do not pronounce the words.

Reading
- Click the Reading tab for children to see the printed word. Note: Children *are not told* the word. The word is broken down into its constituent phonemes. Ask children to say each of the phonemes in the word.
- Click Blend to watch and hear the Bug's demonstration of how to blend the word.
- Click Undo and then ask a child to come to the Work area and move the arrow along. Encourage the whole class to blend the sounds out loud as the arrow moves along pushing the letters together. We recommend a smooth articulation of the sounds for blending.
- Work through each of the words in sequence. Click ▶ to change words.

Spelling
- The children return to their seats.
- Start by selecting the Words tab. Remember, the children do not see the word. Click Say to hear the word and ask the children to repeat it. Then ask the children to use their magnetic letters to make the word on their own magnetic boards, saying the word every time they look for a letter. Follow the procedure for word spelling on page 47.
- Ask a child to come up to the Work area to make the word. Did everyone get it right?
- Ask a child to use the arrow to push the letters together. Encourage the class to blend the word out loud.
- Repeat for the remaining word under the Words tab.
- Under the Pictures tab, click Show to display the image. You and the children say the picture word and proceed to spell it as before. Repeat if there is more than one image.

Writing
- Ask the children to find the letters 'n' and 'g' among their magnetic letters and to feel the shape of them. Click Show and ask the children to look and listen as the lowercase letters are formed.
- "Skywrite" the letters in the air, and ask the children to do the same as you say how to form the letters.
- Ask children to tell you how to write the letters as you write them on the empty Work area.
- Ask children to try to write the letters themselves using paper and pencil or individual whiteboard and pen.
- Select uppercase and repeat when you think this to be appropriate for your children.

WRAP-UP
- Recap the learning intentions with the children.
- Play the "This is 'ng'" video again, then play the alphabet song and encourage the children to sing along, signifying the end of the session.

Learning intentions are to:
- recap what we know
- say the phoneme /ng/
- find the letters 'ng'
- read words with 'ng' in
- spell words with 'ng' in
- write the letters 'ng'

Focus content: revision

Letters and Sounds
w, x, y, z, zz, qu, ch, sh, th
Reading
with, this, moth, thin
Writing and Spelling
qu, ch, sh, th
that, then, thick, froth

Focus content: lesson

Sounds
"This is 'ng'" video
Visual search
sing, thing, bring, string
Reading
Audio: song, hang, rung, thing
No audio: rang, wing, bring, ping
Spelling
Words tab: sing, long
Pictures tab: king, ring
Writing
ng

Next steps
- Play the online pupil games for Unit 7
- Complete the phoneme PCM for Unit 8 (ng)
- Read Phonics Bug books that practise y, z, zz, qu:
  A Picnic
  Is It Quick?
  Quick! Quick! Quick!
  Quick Quiz
  Sid and Zak
  Slip, Slap, Slop!
  The Fox and the Ducks
  The Hunt
  Zap!

Unit 8

Language session

After: ch, sh, th, ng

INTRODUCTION
- Play the alphabet song twice, once with voice accompaniment, children listening and singing along with accompaniment, and once with children singing along to the music without voice accompaniment.
- Discuss with the children the learning intentions for the day.

IRREGULAR

Reading
- Click Show to display the words, and ask/teach the children how to read them. Click Answer to hear the correct pronunciation.
- Explain that in the word "they", 'ey' sounds like the letter name 'a', pronounced /ai/. In the word "she", 'e' sounds like its letter name, pronounced /ee/.

Spelling
- Click Say to hear the word, and ask the children to repeat it.
- Put the word into a sentence, so that the children understand its meaning, for example, "They are working", "She is happy".
- Ask the children to say the word, help to select the lowercase magnetic letters and drag each letter into its empty box. Ask the children to read the word.
- Repeat for the remaining word.

LESSON

Reading
- Click Show to display the sentence, and ask the children to read it.
- Click Answer to reveal whether they are right.
- Repeat for the remaining sentences.

Spelling
- Click Say to hear the caption and ask the children to repeat it.
- Ask the children to help you to select the lowercase magnetic letters and drag the letters to the empty boxes on the Work area.
- Ask the children to read the caption.
- Repeat the procedure for the remaining captions.

Writing
- The children return to their seats.
- Click Say to hear the caption and ask the children to repeat it.
- Ask the children to tell you how to write the caption on the lines provided.
- Clear the screen. Ask the children to say the caption and try to write it using paper and pencil or individual whiteboard and pen.
- Click Answer to check whether they are right.
- Repeat for the remaining captions.

Follow-up
- Display the partial sentence with a picture taking the place of a missing word (chest). You and the children say the word.
- Ask the children to read the sentence, saying the picture word for the missing word. Spell the word, using paper and pencil.
- Click on the picture itself to show the word.

WRAP-UP
- Recap the learning intentions with the children.
- Play the alphabet song again and encourage the children to sing along, signifying the end of the session.

Learning intentions are to:
- learn to read and spell the irregular words "they" and "she"
- learn to read and spell short captions

Focus content: irregular

Reading
they, she
Spelling
they, she

Focus content: lesson

Reading
Beth and Josh had a chat. She is his chum. They bring cash to the shop.
Spelling
fish and chips, thick and thin, sing a song
Writing
fish and chips, thick and thin, sing a song
Follow-up
Picture shows: chest

Next steps
- Play the online language pupil games for Unit 8
- Complete the language PCM for Unit 8
- Read Phonics Bug books that practise ch, sh, th, ng:
    Chick Gets Lost
    In a Rush
    Mixing Muffins
    Munching Lunch
    No Lunch!
    Sand Champ
    Sharon and Flash
    Sid and Nan Invent The Thing

Unit 9

Target phoneme /ai/ written as 'ai'

INTRODUCTION
- Play the alphabet song twice, once with voice accompaniment, children listening and singing along with accompaniment, and once with children singing along to the music without voice accompaniment.
- Discuss with the children the learning intentions for the day.

REVISION
[previously taught grapheme–phoneme correspondences; blending phonemes for reading; segmenting spoken words for spelling]
- Go through the Revision screens at a brisk pace.
- Watch out for any children who have not remembered the phonemes or the graphemes.

LESSON

Sounds
- Choose the relevant lesson session.
- Play the "This is 'ai'" video once through.
- Say the phoneme /ai/, and ask the children to repeat it after you. Make sure you keep the sound pure and encourage the children to do the same.

Visual Search
- Bring up the words from the asset bank onto the Work area. Ask the children to highlight the 'ai' in each of the words, saying whether ai's position is at the beginning, the middle or the end of the word. Do not pronounce the words.

Reading
- Click the Reading tab for children to see the printed word. Note: Children *are not told* the word. The word is broken down into its constituent phonemes. Ask children to say each of the phonemes in the word.
- Click Blend to watch and hear the Bug's demonstration of how to blend the word.
- Click Undo and then ask a child to come to the Work area and move the arrow along. Encourage the whole class to blend the sounds out loud as the arrow moves along pushing the letters together. We recommend a smooth articulation of the sounds for blending.
- Work through each of the words in sequence. Click ▶ to change words.

Spelling
- The children return to their seats.
- Start by selecting the Words tab. Remember, the children do not see the word. Click Say to hear the word and ask the children to repeat it. Then ask the children to use their magnetic letters to make the word on their own magnetic boards, saying the word every time they look for a letter. Follow the procedure for word spelling on page 47.
- Ask a child to come up to the Work area to make the word. Did everyone get it right?
- Ask a child to use the arrow to push the letters together. Encourage the class to blend the word out loud.
- Repeat for the remaining word under the Words tab.
- Under the Pictures tab, click Show to display the image. You and the children say the picture word and proceed to spell it as before. Repeat if there is more than one image.
- Select the Spelling video and play it once through.

Writing
- Ask the children to find the letters 'a' and 'i' among their magnetic letters and to feel the shape of them. Click Show and ask the children to look and listen as the lowercase letters are formed.
- "Skywrite" the letters in the air, and ask the children to do the same as you say how to form the letters.
- Ask children to tell you how to write the letters as you write them on the empty Work area.
- Ask children to try to write the letters themselves using paper and pencil or individual whiteboard and pen.
- Select uppercase and repeat when you think this to be appropriate for your children.

WRAP-UP
- Recap the learning intentions with the children.
- Play the "This is ai" video again, then play the alphabet song and encourage the children to sing along, signifying the end of the session.

Learning intentions are to:
- recap what we know
- say the phoneme /ai/
- find the letters 'ai'
- read words with 'ai' in
- spell words with 'ai' in
- write the letters 'ai'

Focus content: revision

Letters and Sounds
x, y, z, zz, qu, ch, sh, th, ng
Reading
sing, long, king, ring
Writing and Spelling
ch, sh, th, ng
rang, wing, bring, ping

Focus content: lesson

Sounds
"This is 'ai'" video
Visual search
aim, mail, paid, rail
Reading
Audio: aim, mail, paid, rail
No audio: sail, wait, main, train
Spelling
Words tab: rain, tail
Pictures tab: nail, snail
Video: rain, trail
Writing
ai

Next steps
- Play the online pupil games for Unit 8
- Complete the phoneme PCM for Unit 9 (ai)
- Read Phonics Bug books that practise ch, sh, th, ng:
    Chick Gets Lost
    In a Rush
    Mixing Muffins
    Munching Lunch
    No Lunch!
    Sand Champ
    Sharon and Flash
    Sid and Nan Invent
    The Thing

Unit 9

Target phoneme /ee/ written as 'ee'

INTRODUCTION
- Play the alphabet song twice, once with voice accompaniment, children listening and singing along with accompaniment, and once with children singing along to the music without voice accompaniment.
- Discuss with the children the learning intentions for the day.

REVISION
[previously taught grapheme–phoneme correspondences; blending phonemes for reading; segmenting spoken words for spelling]
- Go through the Revision screens at a brisk pace.
- Watch out for any children who have not remembered the phonemes or the graphemes.

LESSON

Sounds
- Choose the relevant lesson session.
- Play the "This is 'ee'" video once through.
- Say the phoneme /ee/, and ask the children to repeat it after you. Make sure you keep the sound pure and encourage the children to do the same.

Visual Search
- Bring up the words from the asset bank onto the Work area. Ask the children to highlight the 'ee' in each of the words, saying whether ee's position is at the beginning, the middle or the end of the word. Do not pronounce the words.

Reading
- Click the Reading tab for children to see the printed word. Note: Children *are not told* the word. The word is broken down into its constituent phonemes. Ask children to say each of the phonemes in the word.
- Click Blend to watch and hear the Bug's demonstration of how to blend the word.
- Click Undo and then ask a child to come to the Work area and move the arrow along. Encourage the whole class to blend the sounds out loud as the arrow moves along pushing the letters together. We recommend a smooth articulation of the sounds for blending.
- Work through each of the words in sequence. Click ▶ to change words.

Spelling
- The children return to their seats.
- Start by selecting the Words tab. Remember, the children do not see the word. Click Say to hear the word and ask the children to repeat it. Then ask the children to use their magnetic letters to make the word on their own magnetic boards, saying the word every time they look for a letter. Follow the procedure for word spelling on page 47.
- Ask a child to come up to the Work area to make the word. Did everyone get it right?
- Ask a child to use the arrow to push the letters together. Encourage the class to blend the word out loud.
- Repeat for the remaining word under the Words tab.
- Under the Pictures tab, click Show to display the image. You and the children say the picture word and proceed to spell it as before. Repeat if there is more than one image.
- Select the Spelling video and play it once through.

Writing
- Ask the children to find the letter 'e' among their magnetic letters and to feel the shape of it. Click Show and ask the children to look and listen as the lowercase letters are formed.
- "Skywrite" the letters in the air, and ask the children to do the same as you say how to form the letters.
- Ask children to tell you how to write the letters as you write them on the empty Work area.
- Ask children to try to write the letters themselves using paper and pencil or individual whiteboard and pen.
- Select uppercase and repeat when you think this to be appropriate for your children.

WRAP-UP
- Recap the learning intentions with the children.
- Play the "This is 'ee'" video again, then play the alphabet song and encourage the children to sing along, signifying the end of the session.

Learning intentions are to:
- recap what we know
- say the phoneme /ee/
- find the letters 'ee'
- read words with 'ee' in
- spell words with 'ee' in
- write the letters 'ee'

Focus content: revision

Letters and Sounds
y, z, zz, qu, ch, sh, th, ng, ai
Reading
rain, tail, nail, snail
Writing and Spelling
sh, th, ng, ai
sail, wait, main, train

Focus content: lesson

Sounds
"This is 'ee'" video
Visual search
eel, teeth, bee, sheep
Reading
Audio: eel, teeth, seem, sheep
No audio: peel, tree, see, sleep
Spelling
Words tab: green, feet
Pictures tab: sheep, bee
Video: seed, tree
Writing
ee

Next steps
- Play the online pupil games for Unit 8
- Complete the phoneme PCM for Unit 9 (ee)
- Read Phonics Bug books that practise ch, sh, th, ng:
    Chick Gets Lost
    In a Rush
    Mixing Muffins
    Munching Lunch
    No Lunch!
    Sand Champ
    Sharon and Flash
    Sid and Nan Invent
    The Thing

Unit 9

Target phoneme /igh/ written as 'igh'

INTRODUCTION
- Play the alphabet song twice, once with voice accompaniment, children listening and singing along with accompaniment, and once with children singing along to the music without voice accompaniment.
- Discuss with the children the learning intentions for the day.

REVISION
[previously taught grapheme–phoneme correspondences; blending phonemes for reading; segmenting spoken words for spelling]
- Go through the Revision screens at a brisk pace.
- Watch out for any children who have not remembered the phonemes or the graphemes.

LESSON

Sounds
- Choose the relevant lesson session.
- Select and drag the trigraph 'igh' on to the Work area. Click on the trigraph to hear how to say the phoneme /igh/.
- Say the phoneme /igh/, and ask the children to repeat it after you. Make sure you keep the sound pure and encourage the children to do the same.

Visual Search
- Bring up the words from the asset bank onto the Work area. Ask the children to highlight the 'igh' in each of the words, saying whether igh's position is at the beginning, the middle or the end of the word. Do not pronounce the words.

Reading
- Click the Reading tab for children to see the printed word. Note: Children *are not told* the word. The word is broken down into its constituent phonemes. Ask children to say each of the phonemes in the word.
- Click Blend to watch and hear the Bug's demonstration of how to blend the word.
- Click Undo and then ask a child to come to the Work area and move the arrow along. Encourage the whole class to blend the sounds out loud as the arrow moves along pushing the letters together. We recommend a smooth articulation of the sounds for blending.
- Work through each of the words in sequence. Click ▶ to change words.

Spelling
- The children return to their seats.
- Start by selecting the Words tab. Remember, the children do not see the word. Click Say to hear the word and ask the children to repeat it. Then ask the children to use their magnetic letters to make the word on their own magnetic boards, saying the word every time they look for a letter. Follow the procedure for word spelling on page 47.
- Ask a child to come up to the Work area to make the word. Did everyone get it right?
- Ask a child to use the arrow to push the letters together. Encourage the class to blend the word out loud.
- Repeat for the remaining word under the Words tab.
- Under the Pictures tab, click Show to display the image. You and the children say the picture word and proceed to spell it as before. Repeat if there is more than one image.

Writing
- Ask the children to find the letters 'i', 'g' and 'h' among their magnetic letters and to feel the shape of them. Click Show and ask the children to look and listen as the lowercase letters are formed.
- "Skywrite" the letters in the air, and ask the children to do the same as you say how to form the letters.
- Ask children to tell you how to write the letters as you write them on the empty Work area.
- Ask children to try to write the letters themselves using paper and pencil or individual whiteboard and pen.
- Select uppercase and repeat when you think this to be appropriate for your children.

WRAP-UP
- Recap the learning intentions with the children.
- Play the alphabet song and encourage the children to sing along, signifying the end of the session.

Learning intentions are to:
- recap what we know
- say the phoneme /igh/
- find the letters 'igh'
- read words with 'igh' in
- spell words with 'igh' in
- write the letters 'igh'

Focus content: revision

Letters and Sounds
z, zz, qu, ch, sh, th, ng, ai, ee
Reading
green, feet, sheep, bee
Writing and Spelling
th, ng, ai, ee
peel, tree, see, sleep

Focus content: lesson

Sounds
/igh/
Visual search
high, sight, might, fright
Reading
Audio: high, sight, might, fright
No audio: sigh, right, bright, tonight
Spelling
Words tab: fight, flight
Pictures tab: light, night
Writing
igh

Next steps
- Play the online pupil games for Unit 8
- Complete the phoneme PCM for Unit 9 (igh)
- Read Phonics Bug books that practise ch, sh, th, ng:
    Chick Gets Lost
    In a Rush
    Mixing Muffins
    Munching Lunch
    No Lunch!
    Sand Champ
    Sharon and Flash
    Sid and Nan Invent The Thing

Unit 9

Target phoneme /oa/ written as 'oa'

INTRODUCTION
- Play the alphabet song twice, once with voice accompaniment, children listening and singing along with accompaniment, and once with children singing along to the music without voice accompaniment.
- Discuss with the children the learning intentions for the day.

REVISION
[previously taught grapheme–phoneme correspondences; blending phonemes for reading; segmenting spoken words for spelling]
- Go through the Revision screens at a brisk pace.
- Watch out for any children who have not remembered the phonemes or the graphemes.

LESSON

Sounds
- Choose the relevant lesson session.
- Explain to the children that 'oa' is used at the beginning or middle of a word.
- Play the "This is 'oa'" video once through.
- Say the phoneme /oa/, and ask the children to repeat it after you. Make sure you keep the sound pure and encourage the children to do the same.

Visual Search
- Bring up the words from the asset bank onto the Work area. Ask the children to highlight the 'oa' in each of the words, saying whether oa's position is at the beginning, the middle or the end of the word. Do not pronounce the words.

Reading
- Click the Reading tab for children to see the printed word. Note: Children *are not told* the word. The word is broken down into its constituent phonemes. Ask children to say each of the phonemes in the word.
- Click Blend to watch and hear the Bug's demonstration of how to blend the word.
- Click Undo and then ask a child to come to the Work area and move the arrow along. Encourage the whole class to blend the sounds out loud as the arrow moves along pushing the letters together. We recommend a smooth articulation of the sounds for blending.
- Work through each of the words in sequence. Click ▶ to change words.

Spelling
- The children return to their seats.
- Start by selecting the Words tab. Remember, the children do not see the word. Click Say to hear the word and ask the children to repeat it. Then ask the children to use their magnetic letters to make the word on their own magnetic boards, saying the word every time they look for a letter. Follow the procedure for word spelling on page 47.
- Ask a child to come up to the Work area to make the word. Did everyone get it right?
- Ask a child to use the arrow to push the letters together. Encourage the class to blend the word out loud.
- Repeat for the remaining word under the Words tab.
- Under the Pictures tab, click Show to display the image. You and the children say the picture word and proceed to spell it as before. Repeat if there is more than one image.
- Select the Spelling video and play it once through.

Writing
- Ask the children to find the letters 'o' and 'a' among their magnetic letters and to feel the shape of them. Click Show and ask the children to look and listen as the lowercase letters are formed.
- "Skywrite" the letters in the air, and ask the children to do the same as you say how to form the letters.
- Ask children to tell you how to write the letters as you write them on the empty Work area.
- Ask children to try to write the letters themselves using paper and pencil or individual whiteboard and pen.
- Select uppercase and repeat when you think this to be appropriate for your children.

WRAP-UP
- Recap the learning intentions with the children.
- Play the "This is 'oa'" video again, then play the alphabet song and encourage children to sing along, signifying the end of the session.

Learning intentions are to:
- recap what we know
- say the phoneme /oa/
- find the letters 'oa'
- read words with 'oa' in
- spell words with 'oa' in
- write the letters 'oa'

Focus content: revision

Letters and Sounds
qu, ch, sh, th, ng, ai, ee, igh

Reading
fight, flight, night, light

Writing and Spelling
ng, ai, ee, igh
sigh, right, bright, tonight

Focus content: lesson

Sounds
"This is 'oa'" video

Visual search

oak, oats, coat, road

Reading
Audio: oak, oats, coat, road
No audio: soap, float, Joan, boatman

Spelling
Words tab: foam, loaf
Pictures tab: goat, toad
Video: loads, coast

Writing
oa

Next steps
- Play the online pupil games for Unit 8
- Complete the phoneme PCM for Unit 9 (oa)
- Read Phonics Bug books that practise ch, sh, th, ng:
  - Chick Gets Lost
  - In a Rush
  - Mixing Muffins
  - Munching Lunch
  - No Lunch!
  - Sand Champ
  - Sharon and Flash
  - Sid and Nan Invent The Thing

Unit 9

Target phoneme /oo/ (long) written as 'oo'

INTRODUCTION
- Play the alphabet song twice, once with voice accompaniment, children listening and singing along with accompaniment, and once with children singing along to the music without voice accompaniment.
- Discuss with the children the learning intentions for the day.

REVISION
[previously taught grapheme–phoneme correspondences; blending phonemes for reading; segmenting spoken words for spelling]
- Go through the Revision screens at a brisk pace.
- Watch out for any children who have not remembered the phonemes or the graphemes.

LESSON

Sounds
- Choose the relevant lesson session. If necessary for your regional accent, point out that /oo/ is pronounced differently in some words.
- Play the "This is 'oo'" video once through.
- Say the phoneme /oo/, and ask the children to repeat it after you. Make sure you keep the sound pure and encourage the children to do the same.

Visual Search
- Bring up the words from the asset bank onto the Work area. Ask the children to highlight the 'oo' in each of the words, saying whether oo's position is at the beginning, the middle or the end of the word. Do not pronounce the words.

Reading
- Click the Reading tab for children to see the printed word. Note: Children *are not told* the word. The word is broken down into its constituent phonemes. Ask children to say each of the phonemes in the word.
- Click Blend to watch and hear the Bug's demonstration of how to blend the word.
- Click Undo and then ask a child to come to the Work area and move the arrow along. Encourage the whole class to blend the sounds out loud as the arrow moves along pushing the letters together. We recommend a smooth articulation of the sounds for blending.
- Work through each of the words in sequence. Click ▶ to change words.

Spelling
- The children return to their seats.
- Start by selecting the Words tab. Remember, the children do not see the word. Click Say to hear the word and ask the children to repeat it. Then ask the children to use their magnetic letters to make the word on their own magnetic boards, saying the word every time they look for a letter. Follow the procedure for word spelling on page 47.
- Ask a child to come up to the Work area to make the word. Did everyone get it right?
- Ask a child to use the arrow to push the letters together. Encourage the class to blend the word out loud.
- Repeat for the remaining word under the Words tab.
- Under the Pictures tab, click Show to display the image. You and the children say the picture word and proceed to spell it as before. Repeat if there is more than one image.
- Select the Spelling video and play it once through.

Writing
- Ask the children to find the letter 'o' among their magnetic letters and to feel the shape of it. Click Show and ask the children to look and listen as the lowercase letters are formed.
- "Skywrite" the letters in the air, and ask the children to do the same as you say how to form the letters.
- Ask children to tell you how to write the letters as you write them on the empty Work area.
- Ask children to try to write the letters themselves using paper and pencil or individual whiteboard and pen.
- Select uppercase and repeat when you think this to be appropriate for your children.

WRAP-UP
- Recap the learning intentions with the children.
- Play the "This is 'oo'" video again, then play the alphabet song and encourage the children to sing along, signifying the end of the session.

Learning intentions are to:
- recap what we know
- say the phoneme /oo/
- find the letters 'oo'
- read words with 'oo' in
- spell words with 'oo' in
- write the letters 'oo'

Focus content: revision

Letters and Sounds
ch, sh, th, ng, ai, ee, igh, oa
Reading
foam, loaf, goat, toad
Writing and Spelling
ai, ee, igh, oa
soap, float, Joan, boatman

Focus content: lesson

Sounds
"This is 'oo'" video
Visual search
zoo, food, moo, spoon
Reading
Audio: zoo, food, moo, boot
No audio: too, moon, cool, pool
Spelling
Words tab: fool, stool
Pictures tab: spoon, roof
Video: hoop, broom
Writing
oo

Next steps
- Play the online pupil games for Unit 8
- Complete the phoneme PCM for Unit 9 (oo)
- Read Phonics Bug books that practise ch, sh, th, ng:
    Chick Gets Lost
    In a Rush
    Mixing Muffins
    Munching Lunch
    No Lunch!
    Sand Champ
    Sharon and Flash
    Sid and Nan Invent
    The Thing

Unit 9

Target phoneme /oo/ (short) written as 'oo'

INTRODUCTION
- Play the alphabet song twice, once with voice accompaniment, children listening and singing along with accompaniment, and once with children singing along to the music without voice accompaniment.
- Discuss with the children the learning intentions for the day.

REVISION
[previously taught grapheme–phoneme correspondences; blending phonemes for reading; segmenting spoken words for spelling]
- Go through the Revision screens at a brisk pace.
- Watch out for any children who have not remembered the phonemes or the graphemes.

LESSON

Sounds
- Choose the relevant lesson session. If necessary for your regional accent, point out that /oo/ is pronounced differently in some words.
- Play the "This is 'oo'" video once through.
- Say the phoneme /oo/, and ask the children to repeat it after you. Make sure you keep the sound pure and encourage the children to do the same.

Visual Search
- Bring up the words from the asset bank onto the Work area. Ask the children to highlight the 'oo' in each of the words, saying whether oo's position is at the beginning, the middle or the end of the word. Do not pronounce the words.

Reading
- Click the Reading tab for children to see the printed word. Note: Children *are not told* the word. The word is broken down into its constituent phonemes. Ask children to say each of the phonemes in the word.
- Click Blend to watch and hear the Bug's demonstration of how to blend the word.
- Click Undo and then ask a child to come to the Work area and move the arrow along. Encourage the whole class to blend the sounds out loud as the arrow moves along pushing the letters together. We recommend a smooth articulation of the sounds for blending.
- Work through each of the words in sequence. Click ▶ to change words.

Spelling
- The children return to their seats.
- Start by selecting the Words tab. Remember, the children do not see the word. Click Say to hear the word and ask the children to repeat it. Then ask the children to use their magnetic letters to make the word on their own magnetic boards, saying the word every time they look for a letter. Follow the procedure for word spelling on page 47.
- Ask a child to come up to the Work area to make the word. Did everyone get it right?
- Ask a child to use the arrow to push the letters together. Encourage the class to blend the word out loud.
- Repeat for the remaining word under the Words tab.
- Under the Pictures tab, click Show to display the image. You and the children say the picture word and proceed to spell it as before. Repeat if there is more than one image.
- Select the Spelling video and play it once through.

Writing
- Ask the children to find the letter 'o' among their magnetic letters and to feel the shape of it. Click Show and ask the children to look and listen as the lowercase letters are formed.
- "Skywrite" the letters in the air, and ask the children to do the same as you say how to form the letters.
- Ask children to tell you how to write the letters as you write them on the empty Work area.
- Ask children to try to write the letters themselves using paper and pencil or individual whiteboard and pen.
- Select uppercase and repeat when you think this to be appropriate for your children.

WRAP-UP
- Recap the learning intentions with the children.
- Play the "This is 'oo'" video again, then play the alphabet song and encourage the children to sing along, signifying the end of the session.

Learning intentions are to:
- recap what we know
- say the phoneme /oo/
- find the letters 'oo'
- read words with 'oo' in
- spell words with 'oo' in
- write the letters 'oo'

Focus content: revision

Letters and Sounds
sh, th, ng, ai, ee, igh, oa, oo
Reading
fool, stool, spoon, roof
Writing and Spelling
ee, igh, oa, oo
too, moon, cool, pool

Focus content: lesson

Sounds
"This is 'oo'" video
Visual search
cook, good, hood, wood
Reading
Audio: cook, good, hood, hook
No audio: look, foot, stood, shook
Spelling
Words tab: took, wool
Pictures tab: book, wood
Video: shook, brook
Writing
oo

Next steps
- Play the online pupil games for Unit 8
- Complete the phoneme PCM for Unit 9 (oo)
- Read Phonics Bug books that practise ch, sh, th, ng:
  Chick Gets Lost
  In a Rush
  Mixing Muffins
  Munching Lunch
  No Lunch!
  Sand Champ
  Sharon and Flash
  Sid and Nan Invent The Thing

Language session

After: ai, ee, igh, oa, oo (long and short)

INTRODUCTION
- Play the alphabet song twice, once with voice accompaniment, children listening and singing along with accompaniment, and once with children singing along to the music without voice accompaniment.
- Discuss with the children the learning intentions for the day.

IRREGULAR

Reading
- Click Show to display the words, and ask/teach the children how to read them. Click Answer to hear the correct pronunciation.
- Explain that in the word "we", 'e' sounds like the letter name, pronounced /ee/. In the word "are", the 'e' is silent but is needed for spelling. Remind the children to look out for silent 'e' words.

Spelling
- Click Say to hear the word, and ask the children to repeat it.
- Put the word into a sentence, so that the children understand its meaning, for example, "We like bananas", "Apples are tasty".
- Ask the children to say the word, help to select the lowercase magnetic letters and drag each letter into its empty box.
- Ask the children to read the word.
- Repeat for the remaining word.

LESSON

Reading
- Click Show to display the sentence, and ask the children to read it.
- Click Answer to reveal whether they are right.
- Repeat for the remaining sentences.

Spelling
- Click Say to hear the caption and ask the children to repeat it.
- Ask the children to help you to select the lowercase magnetic letters and drag the letters to the empty boxes on the Work area.
- Ask the children to read the caption.
- Repeat the procedure for the remaining captions.

Writing
- The children return to their seats.
- Click Say to hear the caption and ask the children to repeat it.
- Ask the children to tell you how to write the caption on the lines provided.
- Clear the screen. Ask the children to say the caption and try to write it using paper and pencil or individual whiteboard and pen.
- Click Answer to check whether they are right.
- Repeat for the remaining captions.

Follow-up
- Display the picture and click on it to show the word (boat). Ask the children to read it.
- Ask the children prompt questions, e.g. "What do you see in the picture? Who would like to take a trip in the boat? Where would you like to go?".
- Ask the children to help you write a sentence about the picture.

WRAP-UP
- Recap the learning intentions with the children.
- Play the alphabet song again and encourage the children to sing along, signifying the end of the session.

Learning intentions are to:
- learn to read and spell the irregular words "we" and "are"
- learn to read and spell short captions

Focus content: irregular

Reading
we, are

Spelling
we, are

Focus content: lesson

Reading
Can we go to the zoo? Yes, we are free this week. Joan might go with us.

Spelling
footstool, aim high, a bee by the tree

Writing
footstool, aim high, a bee by the tree

Follow-up
Picture shows: boat

Next steps
- Play the online language pupil games for Unit 9
- Complete the language PCM for Unit 9
- Read Phonics Bug books that practise ai, ee, igh, oa, oo (long), oo (short):
  - Go, Boat, Go!
  - Go Fish!
  - Meet Zinzan
  - On the Go
  - On the Moon
  - Pandas
  - Rock-pooling
  - The Queen's Plan
  - This Floats, That Sinks

Unit 10

Target phoneme /ar/ written as 'ar'

INTRODUCTION
- Play the alphabet song twice, once with voice accompaniment, children listening and singing along with accompaniment, and once with children singing along to the music without voice accompaniment.
- Discuss with the children the learning intentions for the day.

REVISION
[previously taught grapheme–phoneme correspondences; blending phonemes for reading; segmenting spoken words for spelling]
- Go through the Revision screens at a brisk pace.
- Watch out for any children who have not remembered the phonemes or the graphemes.

LESSON

Sounds
- Choose the relevant lesson session. Explain to the children (if appropriate for their accents) that some words may have the /ar/ sound but there is no 'r' in the spelling, e.g. "father", "rather", "bath", "grass", "fast", "pass".
- Play the "This is 'ar'" video once through.
- Say the phoneme /ar/, and ask the children to repeat it after you. Make sure you keep the sound pure and encourage the children to do the same. (NB: 'ar' is two phonemes in Scotland.)

Visual Search
- Bring up the words from the asset bank onto the Work area. Ask the children to highlight the 'ar' in each of the words, saying whether ar's position is at the beginning, the middle or the end of the word. Do not pronounce the words.

Reading
- Click the Reading tab for children to see the printed word. Note: Children *are not told* the word. The word is broken down into its constituent phonemes. Ask children to say each of the phonemes in the word.
- Click Blend to watch and hear the Bug's demonstration of how to blend the word.
- Click Undo and then ask a child to come to the Work area and move the arrow along. Encourage the whole class to blend the sounds out loud as the arrow moves along pushing the letters together. We recommend a smooth articulation of the sounds for blending.
- Work through each of the words in sequence. Click ▶ to change words.

Spelling
- The children return to their seats.
- Start by selecting the Words tab. Remember, the children do not see the word. Click Say to hear the word and ask the children to repeat it. Then ask the children to use their magnetic letters to make the word on their own magnetic boards, saying the word every time they look for a letter. Follow the procedure for word spelling on page 47.
- Ask a child to come up to the Work area to make the word. Did everyone get it right?
- Ask a child to use the arrow to push the letters together. Encourage the class to blend the word out loud.
- Repeat for the remaining word under the Words tab.
- Under the Pictures tab, click Show to display the image. You and the children say the picture word and proceed to spell it as before. Repeat if there is more than one image.
- Select the Spelling video and play it once through.

Writing
- Ask the children to find the letters 'a' and 'r' among their magnetic letters and to feel the shape of them. Click Show and ask the children to look and listen as the lowercase letters are formed.
- "Skywrite" the letters in the air, and ask the children to do the same as you say how to form the letters.
- Ask children to tell you how to write the letters as you write them on the empty Work area.
- Ask children to try to write the letters themselves using paper and pencil or individual whiteboard and pen.
- Select uppercase and repeat when you think this to be appropriate for your children.

WRAP-UP
- Recap the learning intentions with the children.
- Play the "This is 'ar'" video again, then play the alphabet song and encourage the children to sing along, signifying the end of the session.

Learning intentions are to:
- recap what we know
- say the phoneme /ar/
- find the letters 'ar'
- read words with 'ar' in
- spell words with 'ar' in
- write the letters 'ar'

Focus content: revision

Letters and Sounds
th, ng, ai, ee, igh, oa, oo
Reading
took, wool, book, wood
Writing and Spelling
ee, igh, oa, oo
look, foot, stood, shook

Focus content: lesson

Sounds
"This is 'ar'" video
Visual search
arm, art, jar, start
Reading
Audio: art, jar, park, start
No audio: arch, far, shark, mark
Spelling
Words tab: dart, bark
Pictures tab: arm, star
Video: harp, charm
Writing
ar

Next steps
- Play the online pupil games for Unit 9
- Complete the phoneme PCM for Unit 10 (ar)
- Read Phonics Bug books that practise ai, ee, igh, oa, oo, oo:
  Go, Boat, Go!
  Go Fish!
  Meet Zinzan
  On the Go
  On the Moon
  Pandas
  Rock-pooling
  The Queen's Plan
  This Floats, That Sinks

Unit 10

Target phoneme /or/ written as 'or'

INTRODUCTION
- Play the alphabet song twice, once with voice accompaniment, children listening and singing along with accompaniment, and once with children singing along to the music without voice accompaniment.
- Discuss with the children the learning intentions for the day.

REVISION
[previously taught grapheme–phoneme correspondences; blending phonemes for reading; segmenting spoken words for spelling]
- Go through the Revision screens at a brisk pace.
- Watch out for any children who have not remembered the phonemes or the graphemes.

LESSON
Sounds
- Choose the relevant lesson session.
- Play the "This is 'or'" video once through.
- Say the phoneme /or/, and ask the children to repeat it after you. Make sure you keep the sound pure and encourage the children to do the same. (NB: 'or' is two phonemes in Scotland.)

Visual Search
- Bring up the words from the asset bank onto the Work area. Ask the children to highlight the 'or' in each of the words, saying whether or's position is at the beginning, the middle or the end of the word. Do not pronounce the words.

Reading
- Click the Reading tab for children to see the printed word. Note: Children *are not told* the word. The word is broken down into its constituent phonemes. Ask children to say each of the phonemes in the word.
- Click Blend to watch and hear the Bug's demonstration of how to blend the word.
- Click Undo and then ask a child to come to the Work area and move the arrow along. Encourage the whole class to blend the sounds out loud as the arrow moves along pushing the letters together. We recommend a smooth articulation of the sounds for blending.
- Work through each of the words in sequence. Click ▶ to change words.

Spelling
- The children return to their seats.
- Start by selecting the Words tab. Remember, the children do not see the word. Click Say to hear the word and ask the children to repeat it. Then ask the children to use their magnetic letters to make the word on their own magnetic boards, saying the word every time they look for a letter. Follow the procedure for word spelling on page 47.
- Ask a child to come up to the Work area to make the word. Did everyone get it right?
- Ask a child to use the arrow to push the letters together. Encourage the class to blend the word out loud.
- Repeat for the remaining word under the Words tab.
- Under the Pictures tab, click Show to display the image. You and the children say the picture word and proceed to spell it as before. Repeat if there is more than one image.
- Select the Spelling video and play it once through.

Writing
- Ask the children to find the letters 'o' and 'r' among their magnetic letters and to feel the shape of them. Click Show and ask the children to look and listen as the lowercase letters are formed.
- "Skywrite" the letters in the air, and ask the children to do the same as you say how to form the letters.
- Ask children to tell you how to write the letters as you write them on the empty Work area.
- Ask children to try to write the letters themselves using paper and pencil or individual whiteboard and pen.
- Select uppercase and repeat when you think this to be appropriate for your children.

WRAP-UP
- Recap the learning intentions with the children.
- Play the "This is 'or'" video again, then play the alphabet song and encourage the children to sing along, signifying the end of the session.

Learning intentions are to:
- recap what we know
- say the phoneme /or/
- find the letters 'or'
- read words with 'or' in
- spell words with 'or' in
- write the letters 'or'

Focus content: revision

Letters and Sounds
ng, ai, ee, igh, oa, oo, ar
Reading
dart, bark, arm, star
Writing and Spelling
igh, oa, oo, ar
arch, far, shark, mark

Focus content: lesson

Sounds
"This is 'or'" video
Visual search
or, pork, corn, torch
Reading
Audio: for, pork, cord, corn
No audio: born, stork, orbit, storm
Spelling
Words tab: cork, fort
Pictures tab: torch, fork
Video: horn, sport
Writing
or

Next steps
- Play the online pupil games for Unit 9
- Complete the phoneme PCM for Unit 10 (or)
- Read Phonics Bug books that practise ai, ee, igh, oa, oo, oo:
  - Go, Boat, Go!
  - Go Fish!
  - Meet Zinzan
  - On the Go
  - On the Moon
  - Pandas
  - Rock-pooling
  - The Queen's Plan
  - This Floats, That Sinks

Unit 10

Target phoneme /ur/ written as 'ur'

INTRODUCTION
- Play the alphabet song twice, once with voice accompaniment, children listening and singing along with accompaniment, and once with children singing along to the music without voice accompaniment.
- Discuss with the children the learning intentions for the day.

REVISION
[previously taught grapheme–phoneme correspondences; blending phonemes for reading; segmenting spoken words for spelling]
- Go through the Revision screens at a brisk pace.
- Watch out for any children who have not remembered the phonemes or the graphemes.

LESSON

Sounds
- Choose the relevant lesson session.
- Select and drag the digraph 'ur' on to the Work area. Click on the digraph to hear how to say the phoneme /ur/.
- Say the phoneme /ur/, and ask the children to repeat it after you. Make sure you keep the sound pure and encourage the children to do the same. (NB: 'ur' is two phonemes in Scotland.)

Visual Search
- Bring up the words from the asset bank onto the Work area. Ask the children to highlight the 'ur' in each of the words, saying whether ur's position is at the beginning, the middle or the end of the word. Do not pronounce the words.

Reading
- Click the Reading tab for children to see the printed word. Note: Children *are not told* the word. The word is broken down into its constituent phonemes. Ask children to say each of the phonemes in the word.
- Click Blend to watch and hear the Bug's demonstration of how to blend the word.
- Click Undo and then ask a child to come to the Work area and move the arrow along. Encourage the whole class to blend the sounds out loud as the arrow moves along pushing the letters together. We recommend a smooth articulation of the sounds for blending.
- Work through each of the words in sequence. Click ▶ to change words.

Spelling
- The children return to their seats.
- Start by selecting the Words tab. Remember, the children do not see the word. Click Say to hear the word and ask the children to repeat it. Then ask the children to use their magnetic letters to make the word on their own magnetic boards, saying the word every time they look for a letter. Follow the procedure for word spelling on page 47.
- Ask a child to come up to the Work area to make the word. Did everyone get it right?
- Ask a child to use the arrow to push the letters together. Encourage the class to blend the word out loud.
- Repeat for the remaining word under the Words tab.
- Under the Pictures tab, click Show to display the image. You and the children say the picture word and proceed to spell it as before. Repeat if there is more than one image.

Writing
- Ask the children to find the letters 'u' and 'r' among their magnetic letters and to feel the shape of them. Click Show and ask the children to look and listen as the lowercase letters are formed.
- "Skywrite" the letters in the air, and ask the children to do the same as you say how to form the letters.
- Ask children to tell you how to write the letters as you write them on the empty Work area.
- Ask children to try to write the letters themselves using paper and pencil or individual whiteboard and pen.
- Select uppercase and repeat when you think this to be appropriate for your children.

WRAP-UP
- Recap the learning intentions with the children.
- Play the alphabet song and encourage the children to sing along, signifying the end of the session.

Learning intentions are to:
- recap what we know
- say the phoneme /ur/
- find the letters 'ur'
- read words with 'ur' in
- spell words with 'ur' in
- write the letters 'ur'

Focus content: revision

Letters and Sounds
ai, ee, igh, oa, oo, ar, or
Reading
cork, fort, torch, fork
Writing and Spelling
oa, oo, ar, or
born, stork, orbit, storm

Focus content: lesson

Sounds
/ur/
Visual search
fur, burst, hurt, turnip
Reading
Audio: fur, burst, hurt, turnip
No audio: burp, turn, churn, murmur
Spelling
Words tab: curl, turf
Pictures tab: surf, church
Writing
ur

Next steps
- Play the online pupil games for Unit 9
- Complete the phoneme PCM for Unit 10 (ur)
- Read Phonics Bug books that practise ai, ee, igh, oa, oo, oo:
    Go, Boat, Go!
    Go Fish!
    Meet Zinzan
    On the Go
    On the Moon
    Pandas
    Rock-pooling
    The Queen's Plan
    This Floats, That Sinks

Unit 10

Target phoneme /ow/ written as 'ow'

INTRODUCTION
- Play the alphabet song twice, once with voice accompaniment, children listening and singing along with accompaniment, and once with children singing along to the music without voice accompaniment.
- Discuss with the children the learning intentions for the day.

REVISION
[previously taught grapheme–phoneme correspondences; blending phonemes for reading; segmenting spoken words for spelling]
- Go through the Revision screens at a brisk pace.
- Watch out for any children who have not remembered the phonemes or the graphemes.

LESSON
Sounds
- Choose the relevant lesson session. Explain to the children that 'ow' is used at the end of a word and before 'n' or 'l' at the end of a word.
- Select and drag the digraph 'ow' onto the Work area. Click on the digraph to hear how to say the phoneme /ow/.
- Say the phoneme /ow/, and ask the children to repeat it after you. Make sure you keep the sound pure and encourage the children to do the same.
- Explain to the children that 'ow' is used at the end of a word and before 'n' or 'l' at the end of a word.

Visual Search
- Bring up the words from the asset bank onto the Work area. Ask the children to highlight the 'ow' in each of the words, saying whether ow's position is at the beginning, the middle or the end of the word. Do not pronounce the words.

Reading
- Click the Reading tab for children to see the printed word. Note: Children *are not told* the word. The word is broken down into its constituent phonemes. Ask children to say each of the phonemes in the word.
- Click Blend to watch and hear the Bug's demonstration of how to blend the word.
- Click Undo and then ask a child to come to the Work area and move the arrow along. Encourage the whole class to blend the sounds out loud as the arrow moves along pushing the letters together. We recommend a smooth articulation of the sounds for blending.
- Work through each of the words in sequence. Click ▶ to change words.

Spelling
- The children return to their seats.
- Start by selecting the Words tab. Remember, the children do not see the word. Click Say to hear the word and ask the children to repeat it. Then ask the children to use their magnetic letters to make the word on their own magnetic boards, saying the word every time they look for a letter. Follow the procedure for word spelling on page 47.
- Ask a child to come up to the Work area to make the word. Did everyone get it right?
- Ask a child to use the arrow to push the letters together. Encourage the class to blend the word out loud.
- Repeat for the remaining word under the Words tab.
- Under the Pictures tab, click Show to display the image. You and the children say the picture word and proceed to spell it as before. Repeat if there is more than one image.

Writing
- Ask the children to find the letters 'o' and 'w' among their magnetic letters and to feel the shape of them. Click Show and ask the children to look and listen as the lowercase letters are formed.
- "Skywrite" the letters in the air, and ask the children to do the same as you say how to form the letters.
- Ask children to tell you how to write the letters as you write them on the empty Work area.
- Ask children to try to write the letters themselves using paper and pencil or individual whiteboard and pen.
- Select uppercase and repeat when you think this to be appropriate for your children.

WRAP-UP
- Recap the learning intentions with the children.
- Play the alphabet song and encourage the children to sing along, signifying the end of the session.

Learning intentions are to:
- recap what we know
- say the phoneme /ow/
- find the letters 'ow'
- read words with 'ow' in
- spell words with 'ow' in
- write the letters 'ow'

Focus content: revision

Letters and Sounds
ee, igh, oa, oo, ar, or, ur
Reading
curl, turf, surf, church
Writing and Spelling
oo, ar, or, ur
burp, turn, churn, murmur

Focus content: lesson

Sounds
/ow/
Visual search
how, cow, town, growl
Reading
Audio: how, cow, town, growl
No audio: gown, howl, crown, downtown
Spelling
Words tab: now, drown
Pictures tab: owl, clown
Writing
ow

Next steps
- Play the online pupil games for Unit 9
- Complete the phoneme PCM for Unit 10 (ow)
- Read Phonics Bug books that practise ai, ee, igh, oa, oo, oo:
    Go, Boat, Go!
    Go Fish!
    Meet Zinzan
    On the Go
    On the Moon
    Pandas
    Rock-pooling
    The Queen's Plan
    This Floats, That Sinks

Unit 10

Target phoneme /oi/ written as 'oi'

INTRODUCTION
- Play the alphabet song twice, once with voice accompaniment, children listening and singing along with accompaniment, and once with children singing along to the music without voice accompaniment.
- Discuss with the children the learning intentions for the day.

REVISION
[previously taught grapheme–phoneme correspondences; blending phonemes for reading; segmenting spoken words for spelling]
- Go through the Revision screens at a brisk pace.
- Watch out for any children who have not remembered the phonemes or the graphemes.

LESSON

Sounds
- Choose the relevant lesson session.
- Play the "This is 'oi'" video once through.
- Say the phoneme /oi/, and ask the children to repeat it after you. Make sure you keep the sound pure and encourage the children to do the same.

Visual Search
- Bring up the words from the asset bank onto the Work area. Ask the children to highlight the 'oi' in each of the words, saying whether oi's position is at the beginning, the middle or the end of the word. Do not pronounce the words.

Reading
- Click the Reading tab for children to see the printed word. Note: Children *are not told* the word. The word is broken down into its constituent phonemes. Ask children to say each of the phonemes in the word.
- Click Blend to watch and hear the Bug's demonstration of how to blend the word.
- Click Undo and then ask a child to come to the Work area and move the arrow along. Encourage the whole class to blend the sounds out loud as the arrow moves along pushing the letters together. We recommend a smooth articulation of the sounds for blending.
- Work through each of the words in sequence. Click ▶ to change words.

Spelling
- The children return to their seats.
- Start by selecting the Words tab. Remember, the children do not see the word. Click Say to hear the word and ask the children to repeat it. Then ask the children to use their magnetic letters to make the word on their own magnetic boards, saying the word every time they look for a letter. Follow the procedure for word spelling on page 47.
- Ask a child to come up to the Work area to make the word. Did everyone get it right?
- Ask a child to use the arrow to push the letters together. Encourage the class to blend the word out loud.
- Repeat for the remaining word under the Words tab.
- Under the Pictures tab, click Show to display the image. You and the children say the picture word and proceed to spell it as before. Repeat if there is more than one image.
- Select the Spelling video and play it once through.

Writing
- Ask the children to find the letters 'o' and 'i' among their magnetic letters and to feel the shape of them. Click Show and ask the children to look and listen as the lowercase letters are formed.
- "Skywrite" the letters in the air, and ask the children to do the same as you say how to form the letters.
- Ask children to tell you how to write the letters as you write them on the empty Work area.
- Ask children to try to write the letters themselves using paper and pencil or individual whiteboard and pen.
- Select uppercase and repeat when you think this to be appropriate for your children.

WRAP-UP
- Recap the learning intentions with the children.
- Play the "This is 'oi'" video again, then play the alphabet song and encourage the children to sing along, signifying the end of the session.

Learning intentions are to:
- recap what we know
- say the phoneme /oi/
- find the letters 'oi'
- read words with 'oi' in
- spell words with 'oi' in
- write the letters 'oi'

Focus content: revision

Letters and Sounds
igh, oa, oo, ar, or, ur, ow
Reading
now, drown, owl, clown
Writing and Spelling
ar, or, ur, ow
gown, howl, crown, downtown

Focus content: lesson

Sounds
"This is 'oi'" video
Visual search
oil, coin, coil, boil
Reading
Audio: coin, boil, coil, join
No audio: foil, toil, spoil, point
Spelling
Words tab: soil, joint
Pictures tab: oil, coins
Video : coin, soil
Writing
oi

Next steps
- Play the online pupil games for Unit 9
- Complete the phoneme PCM for Unit 10 (oi)
- Read Phonics Bug books that practise ai, ee, igh, oa, oo, oo:
  Go, Boat, Go!
  Go Fish!
  Meet Zinzan
  On the Go
  On the Moon
  Pandas
  Rock-pooling
  The Queen's Plan
  This Floats, That Sinks

Unit 10

Language session

After: ar, or, ur, ow, oi

INTRODUCTION
- Play the alphabet song twice, once with voice accompaniment, children listening and singing along with accompaniment and once with children singing along to the music without voice accompaniment.
- Discuss with the children the learning intentions for the day.

IRREGULAR

Reading
- Click Show to display the words, and ask/teach the children how to read them. Click Answer to hear the correct pronunciation.
- Explain that the word "you" sounds like the letter name 'u'. In the word "her", 'er' may have the schwa sound /ə/, or in some geographical regions the sound /er/.

Spelling
- Click Say to hear the word, and ask the children to repeat it.
- Put the word into a sentence, so that the children understand its meaning, for example, "I am shorter than you", "That is her crayon".
- Ask the children to say the word, help you to select the lowercase magnetic letters and drag each letter into its empty box.
- Ask the children to read the word.
- Repeat for the remaining words.

LESSON

Reading
- Click Show to display the sentence, and ask the children to read it.
- Click Answer to reveal whether they are right.
- Repeat for the remaining sentences.

Spelling
- Click Say to hear the caption and ask the children to repeat it.
- Ask the children to help you to select the lowercase magnetic letters and drag the letters to the empty boxes on the Work area.
- Ask the children to read the caption.
- Repeat the procedure for the remaining captions.

Writing
- The children return to their seats.
- Click Say to hear the caption and ask the children to repeat it.
- Ask the children to tell you how to write the caption on the lines provided.
- Click Answer to see the caption.
- Clear the screen. Click Say to hear the next caption and ask the children to repeat it.
- Ask them to try to write it themselves using paper and pencil or individual whiteboard and pen.
- Click Answer to check whether they are right.
- Repeat for the remaining caption.

NB: Children hear the caption, say the caption, write the caption, check the caption.

Follow-up
- Display the picture and click on it to show the word (owl). Ask the children to read it.
- Ask the children prompt questions, e.g. "What do you see in the picture? Have you ever seen an owl? Why not?".
- Ask the children to help to write a sentence about the picture.

WRAP-UP
- Recap the learning intentions with the children.
- Play the alphabet song again and encourage the children to sing along, signifying the end of the session.

Learning intentions are to:
- learn to read and spell the irregular words "you" and "her"
- learn to read and spell short captions

Focus content: irregular

Reading
you, her

Spelling
you, her

Focus content: lesson

Reading
Lorna hurt her arm.
She fell down in the park.
Can you go to the market for her?

Spelling
brown cow, a jar of jam, coins in her bag

Writing
brown cow, a jar of jam, coins in her bag

Follow-up
Picture shows: owl

Next steps
- Play the online language pupil games for Unit 10
- Complete the language PCM for Unit 10
- Read Phonics Bug books that practise ar, or, ur, ow, oi:
  A Green Lunch
  Brown Fox Tricks Stork
  In the Dark
  Moo! Cluck! Growl!
  On the Farm
  Sid-Cam
  Stop That Popcorn!
  Turnips and Beetroots
  Up to the Stars

Unit 11

Target phoneme /ear/ written as 'ear'

INTRODUCTION
- Play the alphabet song twice, once with voice accompaniment, children listening and singing along with accompaniment, and once with children singing along to the music without voice accompaniment.
- Discuss with the children the learning intentions for the day.

REVISION
[previously taught grapheme–phoneme correspondences; blending phonemes for reading; segmenting spoken words for spelling]
- Go through the Revision screens at a brisk pace.
- Watch out for any children who have not remembered the phonemes or the graphemes.

LESSON
Sounds
- Choose the relevant lesson session.
- Select and drag the trigraph 'ear' on to the Work area. Click on the trigraph to hear how to say the phoneme /ear/.
- Say the phoneme /ear/, and ask the children to repeat it after you. Make sure you keep the sound pure and encourage the children to do the same. (NB: 'ear' is two phonemes in Scotland.)

Visual Search
- Bring up the words from the asset bank onto the Work area. Ask the children to highlight the 'ear' in each of the words, saying whether ear's position is at the beginning, the middle or the end of the word. Do not pronounce the words.

Reading
- Click the Reading tab for children to see the printed word. Note: Children *are not told* the word. The word is broken down into its constituent phonemes. Ask children to say each of the phonemes in the word.
- Click Blend to watch and hear the Bug's demonstration of how to blend the word.
- Click Undo and then ask a child to come to the Work area and move the arrow along. Encourage the whole class to blend the sounds out loud as the arrow moves along pushing the letters together. We recommend a smooth articulation of the sounds for blending.
- Work through each of the words in sequence. Click ▶ to change words.

Spelling
- The children return to their seats.
- Start by selecting the Words tab. Remember, the children do not see the word. Click Say to hear the word and ask the children to repeat it. Then ask the children to use their magnetic letters to make the word on their own magnetic boards, saying the word every time they look for a letter. Follow the procedure for word spelling on page 47.
- Ask a child to come up to the Work area to make the word. Did everyone get it right?
- Ask a child to use the arrow to push the letters together. Encourage the class to blend the word out loud.
- Repeat for the remaining word under the Words tab.
- Under the Pictures tab, click Show to display the image. You and the children say the picture word and proceed to spell it as before. Repeat if there is more than one image.

Writing
- Ask the children to find the letters 'e', 'a' and 'r' among their magnetic letters and to feel the shape of them. Click Show and ask the children to look and listen as the lowercase letters are formed.
- "Skywrite" the letters in the air, and ask the children to do the same as you say how to form the letters.
- Ask children to tell you how to write the letters as you write them on the empty Work area.
- Ask children to try to write the letters themselves using paper and pencil or individual whiteboard and pen.
- Select uppercase and repeat when you think this to be appropriate for your children.

WRAP-UP
- Recap the learning intentions with the children.
- Play the alphabet song and encourage the children to sing along, signifying the end of the session.

Learning intentions are to:
- recap what we know
- say the phoneme /ear/
- find the letters 'ear'
- read words with 'ear' in
- spell words with 'ear' in
- write the letters 'ear'

Focus content: revision

Letters and Sounds
igh, oa, oo, ar, or, ur, ow, oi
Reading
soil, joint, oil, coins
Writing and Spelling
or, ur, ow, oi
foil, toil, spoil, point

Focus content: lesson

Sounds
/ear/
Visual search
dear, fear, hear, beard
Reading
Audio: dear, fear, hear, beard
No audio: gear, spear, smear, earwig
Spelling
Words tab: year, clear
Pictures tab: ear, earring
Writing
ear

Next steps
- Play the online pupil games for Unit 10
- Complete the phoneme PCM for Unit 11 (ear)
- Read Phonics Bug books that practise ar, or, ur, ow, oi:
  A Green Lunch
  Brown Fox Tricks Stork
  In the Dark
  Moo! Cluck! Growl!
  On the Farm
  Sid-Cam
  Stop That Popcorn!
  Turnips and Beetroots
  Up to the Stars

Unit 11

Target phoneme /air/ written as 'air'

INTRODUCTION
- Play the alphabet song twice, once with voice accompaniment, children listening and singing along with accompaniment, and once with children singing along to the music without voice accompaniment.
- Discuss with the children the learning intentions for the day.

REVISION
[previously taught grapheme–phoneme correspondences; blending phonemes for reading; segmenting spoken words for spelling]
- Go through the Revision screens at a brisk pace.
- Watch out for any children who have not remembered the phonemes or the graphemes.

LESSON

Sounds
- Choose the relevant lesson session.
- Select and drag the trigraph 'air' on to the Work area. Click on the trigraph to hear how to say the phoneme /air/.
- Say the phoneme /air/, and ask the children to repeat it after you. Make sure you keep the sound pure and encourage the children to do the same. (NB: 'air' is two phonemes in Scotland.)

Visual Search
- Bring up the words from the asset bank onto the Work area. Ask the children to highlight the 'air' in each of the words, saying whether air's position is at the beginning, the middle or the end of the word. Do not pronounce the words.

Reading
- Click the Reading tab for children to see the printed word. Note: Children *are not told* the word. The word is broken down into its constituent phonemes. Ask children to say each of the phonemes in the word.
- Click Blend to watch and hear the Bug's demonstration of how to blend the word.
- Click Undo and then ask a child to come to the Work area and move the arrow along. Encourage the whole class to blend the sounds out loud as the arrow moves along pushing the letters together. We recommend a smooth articulation of the sounds for blending.
- Work through each of the words in sequence. Click ▶ to change words.

Spelling
- The children return to their seats.
- Start by selecting the Words tab. Remember, the children do not see the word. Click Say to hear the word and ask the children to repeat it. Then ask the children to use their magnetic letters to make the word on their own magnetic boards, saying the word every time they look for a letter. Follow the procedure for word spelling on page 47.
- Ask a child to come up to the Work area to make the word. Did everyone get it right?
- Ask a child to use the arrow to push the letters together. Encourage the class to blend the word out loud.
- Repeat for the remaining word under the Words tab.
- Under the Pictures tab, click Show to display the image. You and the children say the picture word and proceed to spell it as before. Repeat if there is more than one image.

Writing
- Ask children to find the letters 'a', 'i' and 'r' among their magnetic letters and to feel the shape of them. Click Show and ask the children to look and listen as the lowercase letters are formed.
- "Skywrite" the letters in the air, and ask the children to do the same as you say how to form the letters.
- Ask children to tell you how to write the letters as you write them on the empty Work area.
- Ask children to try to write the letters themselves using paper and pencil or individual whiteboard and pen.
- Select uppercase and repeat when you think this to be appropriate for your children.

WRAP-UP
- Recap the learning intentions with the children.
- Play the alphabet song again and encourage the children to sing along, signifying the end of the session.

Learning intentions are to:
- recap what we know
- say the phoneme /air/
- find the letters 'air'
- read words with 'air' in
- spell words with 'air' in
- write the letters 'air'

Focus content: revision

Letters and Sounds
oa, oo, ar, or, ur, ow, oi, ear

Reading
year, clear, ear, earring

Writing and Spelling
ur, ow, oi, ear
gear, spear, smear, earwig

Focus content: lesson

Sounds
/air/

Visual search
air, hair, pair, stair

Reading
Audio: air, hair, pair, stair
No audio: lair, flair, haircut, airmail

Spelling
Words tab: fair, airport
Pictures tab: chair, stairs

Writing
air

Next steps
- Play the online pupil games for Unit 10
- Complete the phoneme PCM for Unit 11 (air)
- Read Phonics Bug books that practise ar, or, ur, ow, oi:
  A Green Lunch
  Brown Fox Tricks Stork
  In the Dark
  Moo! Cluck! Growl!
  On the Farm
  Sid-Cam
  Stop That Popcorn!
  Turnips and Beetroots
  Up to the Stars

Unit 11

Target phoneme /ure/ written as 'ure'

INTRODUCTION
- Play the alphabet song twice, once with voice accompaniment, children listening and singing along with accompaniment, and once with children singing along to the music without voice accompaniment.
- Discuss with the children the learning intentions for the day.

REVISION
[previously taught grapheme–phoneme correspondences; blending phonemes for reading; segmenting spoken words for spelling]
- Go through the Revision screens at a brisk pace.
- Watch out for any children who have not remembered the phonemes or the graphemes.

LESSON
Sounds
- Choose the relevant lesson session.
- Select and drag the trigraph 'ure' on to the Work area. Click on the trigraph to hear how to say the phoneme /ure/.
- Say the phoneme /ure/, and ask the children to repeat it after you. Make sure you keep the sound pure and encourage the children to do the same. (NB: 'ure' is two phonemes in Scotland.)

Visual Search
- Bring up the words from the asset bank onto the Work area. Ask the children to highlight the 'ure' in each of the words, saying whether ure's position is at the beginning, the middle or the end of the word. Do not pronounce the words.

Reading
- Click the Reading tab for children to see the printed word. Note: Children *are not told* the word. The word is broken down into its constituent phonemes. Ask children to say each of the phonemes in the word.
- Click Blend to watch and hear the Bug's demonstration of how to blend the word.
- Click Undo and then ask a child to come to the Work area and move the arrow along. Encourage the whole class to blend the sounds out loud as the arrow moves along pushing the letters together. We recommend a smooth articulation of the sounds for blending.
- Work through each of the words in sequence. Click ▶ to change words.

Spelling
- The children return to their seats.
- Start by selecting the Words tab. Remember, the children do not see the word. Click Say to hear the word and ask the children to repeat it. Then ask the children to use their magnetic letters to make the word on their own magnetic boards, saying the word every time they look for a letter. Follow the procedure for word spelling on page 47.
- Ask a child to come up to the Work area to make the word. Did everyone get it right?
- Ask a child to use the arrow to push the letters together. Encourage the class to blend the word out loud.
- Repeat for the remaining word under the Words tab.
- Under the Pictures tab, click Show to display the image. You and the children say the picture word and proceed to spell it as before. Repeat if there is more than one image.

Writing
- Ask the children to find the letters 'u', 'r' and 'e' among their magnetic letters and to feel the shape of them. Click Show and ask the children to look and listen as the lowercase letters are formed.
- "Skywrite" the letters in the air, and ask the children to do the same as you say how to form the letters.
- Ask children to tell you how to write the letters as you write them on the empty Work area.
- Ask children to try to write the letters themselves using paper and pencil or individual whiteboard and pen.
- Select uppercase and repeat when you think this to be appropriate for your children.

WRAP-UP
- Recap the learning intentions with the children.
- Play the alphabet song and encourage the children to sing along, signifying the end of the session.

Learning intentions are to:
- recap what we know
- say the phoneme /ure/
- find the letters 'ure'
- read words with 'ure' in
- spell words with 'ure' in
- write the letters 'ure'

Focus content: revision

Letters and Sounds
oo, ar, or, ur, ow, oi, ear, air
Reading
fair, airport, chair, stairs
Writing and Spelling
ow, oi, ear, air
lair, flair, haircut, airmail

Focus content: lesson

Sounds
/ure/
Visual search
cure, endure, sure, secure
Reading
Audio: cure, manure, lure, insure
No audio: secure, mature, endure, assure
Spelling
Words tab: pure, sure
Pictures tab: manure, manicure
Writing
ure

Next steps
- Play the online pupil games for Unit 10
- Complete the phoneme PCM for Unit 11 (ure)
- Read Phonics Bug books that practise ar, or, ur, ow, oi:
  A Green Lunch
  Brown Fox Tricks Stork
  In the Dark
  Moo! Cluck! Growl!
  On the Farm
  Sid-Cam
  Stop That Popcorn!
  Turnips and Beetroots
  Up to the Stars

Unit 11

Target phoneme /ur/ written as 'er'

INTRODUCTION
- Play the alphabet song twice, once with voice accompaniment, children listening and singing along with accompaniment, and once with children singing along to the music without voice accompaniment.
- Discuss with the children the learning intentions for the day.

REVISION
[previously taught grapheme–phoneme correspondences; blending phonemes for reading; segmenting spoken words for spelling]
- Go through the Revision screens at a brisk pace.
- Watch out for any children who have not remembered the phonemes or the graphemes.

LESSON
Sounds
- Choose the relevant lesson session.
- Play the "This is 'er'" video once through.
- Say the phoneme /ur/, and ask the children to repeat it after you. Make sure you keep the sound pure and encourage the children to do the same. (NB: 'er' is two phonemes in Scotland.)

Visual Search
- Bring up the words from the asset bank onto the Work area. Ask the children to highlight the 'er' in each of the words, saying whether er's position is at the beginning, the middle or the end of the word. Do not pronounce the words.

Reading
- Click the Reading tab for children to see the printed word. Note: Children *are not told* the word. The word is broken down into its constituent phonemes. Ask children to say each of the phonemes in the word.
- Click Blend to watch and hear the Bug's demonstration of how to blend the word.
- Click Undo and then ask a child to come to the Work area and move the arrow along. Encourage the whole class to blend the sounds out loud as the arrow moves along pushing the letters together. We recommend a smooth articulation of the sounds for blending.
- Work through each of the words in sequence. Click ▶ to change words.

Spelling
- The children return to their seats.
- Start by selecting the Words tab. Remember, the children do not see the word. Click Say to hear the word and ask the children to repeat it. Then ask the children to use their magnetic letters to make the word on their own magnetic boards, saying the word every time they look for a letter. Follow the procedure for word spelling on page 47.
- Ask a child to come up to the Work area to make the word. Did everyone get it right?
- Ask a child to use the arrow to push the letters together. Encourage the class to blend the word out loud.
- Repeat for the remaining word under the Words tab.
- Under the Pictures tab, click Show to display the image. You and the children say the picture word and proceed to spell it as before. Repeat if there is more than one image.

Writing
- Ask the children to find the letters 'e' and 'r' among their magnetic letters and to feel the shape of them. Click Show and ask the children to look and listen as the lowercase letters are formed.
- "Skywrite" the letters in the air, and ask the children to do the same as you say how to form the letters.
- Ask children to tell you how to write the letters as you write them on the empty Work area.
- Ask children to try to write the letters themselves using paper and pencil or individual whiteboard and pen.
- Select uppercase and repeat when you think this to be appropriate for your children.

WRAP-UP
- Recap the learning intentions with the children.
- Play the "This is 'er'" video again, then play the alphabet song and encourage the children to sing along, signifying the end of the session.

Learning intentions are to:
- recap what we know
- say the phoneme /ur/
- find the letters 'er'
- read words with 'er' in
- spell words with 'er' in
- write the letters 'er'

Focus content: revision

Letters and Sounds
ar, or, ur, ow, oi, ear, air, ure

Reading
pure, sure, manure, manicure

Writing and Spelling
oi, ear, air, ure
secure, endure, mature, assure

Focus content: lesson

Sounds
"This is 'er'" video

Visual search
term, kerb, sister, dinner

Reading
Audio: term, kerb, sister, dinner
No audio: father, perch, number, helper

Spelling
Words tab: farmer, letter
Pictures tab: ladder, cooker

Writing
er

Next steps
- Play the online pupil games for Unit 10
- Complete the phoneme PCM for Unit 11 (er)
- Read Phonics Bug books that practise ar, or, ur, ow, oi:
  A Green Lunch
  Brown Fox Tricks Stork
  In the Dark
  Moo! Cluck! Growl!
  On the Farm
  Sid-Cam
  Stop That Popcorn!
  Turnips and Beetroots
  Up to the Stars

Unit 11

Language session

After: ear, air, ure, er

INTRODUCTION
- Play the alphabet song twice, once with voice accompaniment, children listening and singing along with accompaniment, and once with children singing along to the music without voice accompaniment.
- Discuss with the children the learning intentions for the day.

IRREGULAR
Reading
- Click Show to display the words, and ask/teach the children how to read them. Click Answer to hear the correct pronunciation.
- In the words "all" and "was", the 'a' sounds /o/ or /aw/, depending on the geographical region you are in.

Spelling
- Click Say to hear the word, and ask the children to repeat it.
- Put the word into a sentence, so that the children understand its meaning, for example, "The biscuits have all been eaten", "Yesterday I was at home".
- Ask the children to say the word, help to select the lowercase magnetic letters and drag each letter into its empty box.
- Ask the children to read the word.
- Repeat for the remaining words.

LESSON
Reading
- Click Show to display the sentence, and ask the children to read it.
- Click Answer to reveal whether they are right.
- Repeat for the remaining sentences.

Spelling
- Click Say to hear the caption and ask the children to repeat it.
- Ask the children to help you to select the lowercase magnetic letters and drag the letters to the empty boxes on the Work area.
- Ask the children to read the caption.
- Repeat the procedure for the remaining captions.

Writing
- The children return to their seats.
- Click Say to hear the caption and ask the children to repeat it.
- Ask the children to tell you how to write the caption on the lines provided.
- Click Answer to see the caption.
- Clear the screen. Click Say to hear the next caption and ask the children to repeat it.
- Ask them to try to write it themselves using paper and pencil or individual whiteboard and pen.
- Click Answer to check whether they are right.
- Repeat for the remaining caption.

NB: Children hear the caption, say the caption, write the caption, check the caption.

Follow-up
- Display the picture and click on it to show the caption (chair with a broken leg). Ask the children to read it.
- Ask the children prompt questions such as, "What do you see in the picture?" "What has happened to the chair?" "Do you think you can sit on this chair?"
- Encourage the children to compose sentences to describe the picture or ask a question about the picture using words they have learnt in the programme.
- Use one or two of the children's sentences/questions to further the discussion.

WRAP-UP
- Recap the learning intentions with the children.
- Play the alphabet song again and encourage the children to sing along, signifying the end of the session.

Learning intentions are to:
- learn to read and spell the irregular words "all" and "was"
- learn to read and spell short captions
- contribute to discussion

Focus content: irregular

Reading
all, was
Spelling
all, was

Focus content: lesson

Reading
Dear Father
I was glad to hear from you.
We will all wait for you at the airport.
Spelling
all clear, airmail letter, a short haircut
Writing
all clear, airmail letter, a short haircut
Follow-up
Picture shows: chair with a broken leg

Next steps
- Play the online language pupil games for Unit 11
- Complete the language PCM for Unit 11
- Read Phonics Bug books that practise ear, air, ure, er:
  - A Letter from Dorset
  - Dex and the Funfair
  - Eek! A Bug
  - Hair
  - Is it a Monster?
  - Panther and Frog
  - Summer Storm
  - Unfair!
  - Winter

Adjacent consonants (cvcc)

INTRODUCTION
- Play the alphabet song twice, once with voice accompaniment, children listening and singing along with accompaniment, and once with children singing along to the music without voice accompaniment.
- Discuss with the children the learning intentions for the day.

REVISION
- As no new graphemes are taught in Unit 12, Revision is used to consolidate previously taught vowel digraphs.
- Go through the revision screens at a brisk pace.
- Watch out for any children who have not remembered the phonemes or the graphemes.

LESSON
Sounds
NB: As as no new phonemes are being taught here, the Sounds screen is not needed.

Visual Search
NB: This element is omitted as no new graphemes are being taught.

Reading
- Click the Reading tab for children to see the printed word. Note: Children *are not told* the word. The word is broken down into its constituent phonemes. Ask children to say each of the phonemes in the word.
- Click Blend to watch and hear the Bug's demonstration of how to blend the word.
- Click Undo and then ask a child to come to the Work area and move the arrow along. Encourage the whole class to blend the sounds out loud as the arrow moves along pushing the letters together. We recommend a smooth articulation of the sounds for blending.
- Work through each of the words in sequence. Click ▶ to change words.

Spelling
- The children return to their seats.
- Start by selecting the Words tab. Remember, the children do not see the word. Click Say to hear the word and ask the children to repeat it. Then ask the children to use their magnetic letters to make the word on their own magnetic boards, saying the word every time they look for a letter. Follow the procedure for word spelling on page 47.
- Ask a child to come up to the Work area to make the word. Did everyone get it right?
- Ask a child to use the arrow to push the letters together. Encourage the class to blend the word out loud.
- Repeat for the remaining word under the Words tab.
- Under the Pictures tab, click Show to display the image. You and the children say the picture word and proceed to spell it as before. Repeat if there is more than one image.

Writing
NB: As no new graphemes are being taught here, the Writing screen is not needed.

WRAP-UP
- Recap the learning intentions with the children.
- Play the alphabet song and encourage the children to sing along, signifying the end of the session.

Learning intentions are to:
- recap what we know
- read words with adjacent consonants
- spell words with adjacent consonants

Focus content: revision

Letters and Sounds
or, ur, ow, oi, ear, air, ure, er

Reading
farmer, letter, ladder, cooker

Writing and Spelling
ear, air, ure, er
father, perch, number, helper

Focus content: lesson

Reading
Audio: quilt, soft, next, camp
No audio: belt, went, just, help
Spelling
Words tab: tent, jump
Pictures tab: bulb, milk

Next steps
- Play the online pupil games for Unit 11
- Complete the PCM for Unit 12 (cvcc words)
- Read Phonics Bug books that practise ear, air, ure, er:
    A Letter from Dorset
    Dex and the Funfair
    Eek! A Bug
    Hair
    Is it a Monster?
    Panther and Frog
    Summer Storm
    Unfair!
    Winter

Unit 12

Language session 1
After: cvcc words

INTRODUCTION
- Play the alphabet song twice, once with voice accompaniment, children listening and singing along with accompaniment, and once with children singing along to the music without voice accompaniment.
- Discuss with the children the learning intentions for the day.

IRREGULAR
Reading
- Click Show to display the words, and ask/teach the children how to read them. Click Answer to hear the correct pronunciation.
- Explain that in the following words, different letters have different pronunciations:
  - "said" – 'ai' sounds /e/
  - "have" – 'e' is silent but needed for spelling.
  - "like" – 'i' sounds like its letter name; the 'e' is silent but is needed for spelling.
  - "so" – 'o' sounds like its letter name, pronounced /oa/.
  - "do" – the 'o' sounds /oo/

Spelling
- Click Say to hear the word, and ask the children to repeat it.
- Put the word into a sentence, so that the children understand its meaning, for example, "He said 'I like fish'", "I have six pencils", etc.
- Ask the children to say the word, help to select the lowercase magnetic letters and drag each letter into its empty box.
- Ask the children to read the word.
- Repeat for the remaining words.

LESSON
Reading
- Click Show to display the sentence, and ask the children to read it.
- Click Answer to reveal whether they are right.
- Repeat for the remaining sentences. Note that one sentence includes a question.

Spelling
- Click Say to hear the caption and ask the children to repeat it.
- Ask the children to help you to select the lowercase magnetic letters and drag the letters to the empty boxes on the Work area.
- Ask the children to read the caption.
- Repeat the procedure for the remaining captions.

Writing
- The children return to their seats.
- Click Say to hear the caption and ask the children to repeat it.
- Ask the children to tell you how to write the caption on the lines provided.
- Click Answer to see the caption.
- Clear the screen. Click Say to hear the next caption and ask the children to repeat it.
- Ask them to try to write it themselves using paper and pencil or individual whiteboard and pen.
- Click Answer to check whether they are right.
- Repeat for the remaining caption.

NB: Children hear the caption, say the caption, write the caption, check the caption.

Follow-up
- Display the picture and click on it to show the caption (a fish tank). Ask the children to read it.
- Ask the children prompt questions such as, "What do you see in the picture?", "What is in the tank?", "What are the fish doing?"
- Encourage the children to compose sentences to describe the picture or ask a question about the picture using words they have learnt in the programme.
- Use one or two of the children's sentences/questions to further the discussion.

WRAP-UP
- Recap the learning intentions with the children.
- Play the alphabet song again and encourage the children to sing along, signifying the end of the session.

Learning intentions are to:
- learn to read and spell the irregular words "said", "have", "like", "so", "do"
- learn to read and spell short captions
- contribute to discussion

Focus content: irregular

Reading
said, have, like, so, do

Spelling
said, have, like, so, do

Focus content: lesson

Reading
I said, "Do you like plums?" I have three of them. So you can have them for lunch.

Spelling
a crisp crust, jump and swim, spin the top

Writing
a crisp crust, jump and swim, spin the top

Follow-up
Picture shows: a fish tank

Next steps
- Play the online language pupil games for Unit 12
- Complete the language PCM for Unit 12 Session 1
- Read Phonics Bug books that practise ear, air, ure, er:
  - A Letter from Dorset
  - Dex and the Funfair
  - Eek! A Bug
  - Hair
  - Is it a Monster?
  - Panther and Frog
  - Summer Storm
  - Unfair!
  - Winter

Unit 12

Adjacent consonants (ccvc)

INTRODUCTION
- Play the alphabet song twice, once with voice accompaniment, children listening and singing along with accompaniment, and once with children singing along to the music without voice accompaniment.
- Discuss with the children the learning intentions for the day.

REVISION
- As no new graphemes are taught in Unit 12, Revision is used to consolidate previously taught vowel digraphs.
- Go through the revision screens at a brisk pace.
- Watch out for any children who have not remembered the phonemes or the graphemes.

LESSON

Sounds
NB: As no new phonemes are being taught here, the Sounds screen is not needed.

Visual Search
NB: This element is omitted as no new graphemes are being taught.

Reading
- Click the Reading tab for children to see the printed word. Note: Children *are not told* the word. The word is broken down into its constituent phonemes. Ask children to say each of the phonemes in the word.
- Click Blend to watch and hear the Bug's demonstration of how to blend the word.
- Click Undo and then ask a child to come to the Work area and move the arrow along. Encourage the whole class to blend the sounds out loud as the arrow moves along pushing the letters together. We recommend a smooth articulation of the sounds for blending.
- Work through each of the words in sequence. Click ▶ to change words.

Spelling
- The children return to their seats.
- Start by selecting the Words tab. Remember, the children do not see the word. Click Say to hear the word and ask the children to repeat it. Then ask the children to use their magnetic letters to make the word on their own magnetic boards, saying the word every time they look for a letter. Follow the procedure for word spelling on page 47.
- Ask a child to come up to the Work area to make the word. Did everyone get it right?
- Ask a child to use the arrow to push the letters together. Encourage the class to blend the word out loud.
- Repeat for the remaining word under the Words tab.
- Under the Pictures tab, click Show to display the image. You and the children say the picture word and proceed to spell it as before. Repeat if there is more than one image.

Writing
NB: As no new graphemes are being taught here, the Writing screen is not needed.

WRAP-UP
- Recap the learning intentions with the children.
- Play the alphabet song and encourage the children to sing along, signifying the end of the session.

Learning intentions are to:
- recap what we know
- read words with adjacent consonants
- spell words with adjacent consonants

Focus content: revision

Letters and Sounds
ow, oi, ear, air, ure, er
Reading
tent, jump, bulb, milk
Writing and Spelling
air, ure, er
belt, went, just, help

Focus content: lesson

Reading
Audio: blot, clap, crab, stem
No audio: plan, sleep, from, crop
Spelling
Words tab: swim, spin
Pictures tab: pram, dragon

Next steps
- Play the online pupil games for Unit 11
- Complete the PCM for Unit 12 (ccvc words)
- Read Phonics Bug books that practise ear, air, ure, er:
  A Letter from Dorset
  Dex and the Funfair
  Eek! A Bug
  Hair
  Is it a Monster?
  Panther and Frog
  Summer Storm
  Unfair!
  Winter

Unit 12

Language session 2
After: ccvc words

INTRODUCTION
- Play the alphabet song twice, once with voice accompaniment, children listening and singing along with accompaniment, and once with children singing along to the music without voice accompaniment.
- Discuss with the children the learning intentions for the day.

IRREGULAR
Reading
- Click Show to display the words, and ask/teach the children how to read them. Click Answer to hear the correct pronunciation.
- Explain that in the following words, different letters have different pronunciations:
  - "some" and "come" – 'o' sounds /u/; the 'e' is silent but needed for spelling.
  - "were" and "there" – the final 'e' is silent but needed for spelling.
  - "little" – 'le' at the end of a word can sound /ul/.

Spelling
- Click Say to hear the word, and ask the children to repeat it.
- Put the word into a sentence, so that the children understand its meaning, for example, "I would like some strawberries", "Come to my party", etc.
- Ask the children to say the word, help to select the lowercase magnetic letters and drag each letter into its empty box. Ask the children to read the word.
- Repeat for the remaining words.

LESSON
Reading
- Click Show to display the sentence, and ask the children to read it.
- Click Answer to reveal whether they are right.
- Repeat for the remaining sentences. Point out the use of direct speech.

Spelling
- Click Say to hear the caption and ask the children to repeat it.
- Ask the children to help you to select the lowercase magnetic letters and drag the letters to the empty boxes on the Work area.
- Ask the children to read the caption.
- Repeat the procedure for the remaining captions.

Writing
- The children return to their seats.
- Click Say to hear the caption and ask the children to repeat it.
- Ask the children to tell you how to write the caption on the lines provided.
- Click Answer to see the caption.
- Clear the screen. Click Say to hear the next caption and ask the children to repeat it.
- Ask them to try to write it themselves using paper and pencil or individual whiteboard and pen.
- Click Answer to check whether they are right.
- Repeat for the remaining caption.

NB: Children hear the caption, say the caption, write the caption, check the caption.

Follow-up
- Display the picture and click on it to show the caption (bird on a swing). Ask the children to read it.
- Ask the children prompt questions such as "What do you see in the picture?", "What is the bird sitting on?".
- Encourage the children to compose sentences to describe the picture or ask a question about the picture using words they have learnt in the programme.
- Use one or two of the children's sentences/questions to further the discussion.

WRAP-UP
- Recap the learning intentions with the children.
- Play the alphabet song again and encourage the children to sing along, signifying the end of the session.

Learning intentions are to:
- learn to read and spell the irregular words "some", "come", "were", "there" and "little"
- learn to read and spell short captions
- contribute to discussion

Focus content: irregular

Reading
some, come, were, there, little

Spelling
some, come, were, there, little

Focus content: lesson

Reading
There were some big fish in a pond.
A little crab swam up to them. "Can I swim with you?" he said.

Spelling
skim and scan, spilt milk, a strand of hair

Writing
skim and scan, spilt milk, a strand of hair

Follow-up
Picture shows: bird on a swing

Next steps
- Play the online language pupil games for Unit 12
- Complete the language PCM for Unit 12 Session 2
- Read Phonics Bug books that practise ear, air, ure, er:
  A Letter from Dorset
  Dex and the Funfair
  Eek! A Bug
  Hair
  Is it a Monster?
  Panther and Frog
  Summer Storm
  Unfair!
  Winter

Unit 12

Adjacent consonants (ccvcc/cccvc/cccvcc)

INTRODUCTION
- Play the alphabet song twice, once with voice accompaniment, children listening and singing along with accompaniment, and once with children singing along to the music without voice accompaniment.
- Discuss with the children the learning intentions for the day.

REVISION
- As no new graphemes are taught in Unit 12, Revision is used to consolidate previously taught vowel digraphs.
- Go through the revision screens at a brisk pace.
- Watch out for any children who have not remembered the phonemes or the graphemes.

LESSON

Sounds
NB: As no new phonemes are being taught here, the Sounds screen is not needed.

Visual Search
NB: This element is omitted as no new graphemes are being taught.

Reading
- Click the Reading tab for children to see the printed word. Note: Children *are not told* the word. The word is broken down into its constituent phonemes. Ask children to say each of the phonemes in the word.
- Click Blend to watch and hear the Bug's demonstration of how to blend the word.
- Click Undo and then ask a child to come to the Work area and move the arrow along. Encourage the whole class to blend the sounds out loud as the arrow moves along pushing the letters together. We recommend a smooth articulation of the sounds for blending.
- Work through each of the words in sequence. Click ▶ to change words.

Spelling
- The children return to their seats.
- Start by selecting the Words tab. Remember, the children do not see the word. Click Say to hear the word and ask the children to repeat it. Then ask the children to use their magnetic letters to make the word on their own magnetic boards, saying the word every time they look for a letter. Follow the procedure for word spelling on page 47.
- Ask a child to come up to the Work area to make the word. Did everyone get it right?
- Ask a child to use the arrow to push the letters together. Encourage the class to blend the word out loud.
- Repeat for the remaining word under the Words tab.
- Under the Pictures tab, click Show to display the image. You and the children say the picture word and proceed to spell it as before. Repeat if there is more than one image.

Writing
NB: As no new graphemes are being taught here, the Writing screen is not needed.

WRAP-UP
- Recap the learning intentions with the children.
- Play the alphabet song and encourage the children to sing along, signifying the end of the session.

Learning intentions are to:
- recap what we know
- read words with adjacent consonants
- spell words with adjacent consonants

Focus content: revision

Letters and Sounds
ear, air, ure, er

Reading
swim, spin, pram, dragon

Writing and Spelling
ure, er
plan, sleep, from, crop

Focus content: lesson

Reading
Audio: crept, twist, drift, split, splint, bench

No audio: blast, swift, spilt, strap, strand, drench

Spelling
Words tab: crisp, plump

Pictures tab: plant, stamp

Next steps
- Play the online pupil games for Unit 12
- Complete the PCM for Unit 12 (ccvcc words)
- Read Phonics Bug books that practise adjacent consonants:
  A Job for Jim
  A Little Green Monster
  At the Dentist
  Be a Cress Barber
  Cool Cars
  Fantastic Fish
  Look What We Can Do!
  Monsters!
  Pompom Pets
  Sea Fishing
  Sid and the Boxer Pup
  Sid and the Haircut
  Sid Snaps
  Snails
  Springs and Things
  Stop Helping!
  Stuck in a Trap
  The Bright Stars
  There's Something in the Garden
  Trains

Unit 12

Language session 3

After: ccvcc, cccvc and cccvcc words

INTRODUCTION
- Play the alphabet song twice, once with voice accompaniment, children listening and singing along with accompaniment, and once with children singing along to the music without voice accompaniment.
- Discuss with the children the learning intentions for the day.

IRREGULAR

Reading
- Click Show to display the words, and ask/teach the children how to read them. Click Answer to hear the correct pronunciation.
- Explain that in the following words, different letters have different pronunciations:
  - "one" – pronounced 'wun'.
  - "out" – 'ou' sounds /ow/ as in "cow".
  - "what" – 'a' sounds /o/ or /aw/, depending on the geographical region you are in.
- Explain to the children that "what" and "when" are question words.

Spelling
- Click Say to hear the word, and ask the children to repeat it.
- Put the word into a sentence, so that the children understand its meaning, for example, "What are you doing?", "When shall we go out to the farm?".
- Ask the children to say the word, help to select the lowercase magnetic letters and drag each letter into its empty box.
- Ask the children to read the word.
- Repeat for the remaining words.

LESSON

Reading
- Click Show to display the sentence, and ask the children to read it.
- Click Answer to reveal whether they are right.
- Repeat for the remaining sentences. Note that one sentence includes a question.

Spelling
- Click Say to hear the caption and ask the children to repeat it.
- Ask the children to help you to select the lowercase magnetic letters and drag the letters to the empty boxes on the Work area.
- Ask the children to read the caption.
- Repeat the procedure for the remaining captions.

Writing
- The children return to their seats.
- Click Say to hear the caption and ask the children to repeat it.
- Ask the children to tell you how to write the caption on the lines provided.
- Click Answer to see the caption.
- Clear the screen. Click Say to hear the next caption and ask the children to repeat it.
- Ask them to try to write it themselves using paper and pencil or individual whiteboard and pen.
- Click Answer to check whether they are right.
- Repeat for the remaining caption.

NB: Children hear the caption, say the caption, write the caption, check the caption.

Follow-up
- Display the picture and click on it to show the caption (children having a picnic). Ask the children to read it.
- Ask the children prompt questions such as "What do you see in the picture?", "How do you know what the children are doing?", "What would happen if there was a thunderstorm?", "What would the children do next?".
- Encourage the children to compose sentences to describe the picture or ask a question about the picture using words they have learnt in the programme.
- Use one or two of the children's sentences/questions to further the discussion.

WRAP-UP
- Recap the learning intentions with the children.
- Play the alphabet song again and encourage the children to sing along, signifying the end of the session.

Learning intentions are to:
- learn to read and spell the irregular words "one", "when", "out", "what"
- learn to read and spell short captions
- contribute to discussion

Focus content: irregular

Reading
one, when, out, what
Spelling
one, when, out, what

Focus content: lesson

Reading
When the rain stops, we can go out.
One of my boots is split.
What can I do?
Spelling
twist and turn, a soft quilt, a crisp frost
Writing
twist and turn, a soft quilt, a crisp frost
Follow-up
Picture shows: children having a picnic

Next steps
- Play the online language pupil games for Unit 12
- Complete the language PCM for Unit 12 Session 3
- Read Phonics Bug books that practise adjacent consonants:
  A Job for Jim
  A Little Green Monster
  At the Dentist
  Be a Cress Barber
  Cool Cars
  Fantastic Fish
  Look What We Can Do!
  Monsters!
  Pompom Pets
  Sea Fishing
  Sid and the Boxer Pup
  Sid and the Haircut
  Sid Snaps
  Snails
  Springs and Things
  Stop Helping!
  Stuck in a Trap
  The Bright Stars
  There's Something in the Garden
  Trains

a b c d e f g h i
j k l m n o p q r
s t u v w x y z

About the Authors

Dr. Joyce Watson An Early Years teacher for a number of years, she was a lecturer in the Northern College of Education, Dundee, for over 20 years (in Primary Development and Early Education, and in the Psychology Department). She was also a postdoctoral fellow, and an Honorary Research Fellow, in the School of Psychology at the University of St. Andrews for over 10 years. Dr. Watson holds the PGCE Open University Diploma in Reading Development, an M.Ed from the University of Dundee (on reading comprehension), and a Ph.D in Psychology from the University of St. Andrews (on the effects of phonics teaching on children's progress in reading and spelling).

Professor Rhona Johnston A Learning Support teacher for two years, she was in the School of Psychology at the University of St Andrews for 20 years. She was a Reader in the School of Psychology at the University of Birmingham and is now a Professor in the Department of Psychology at the University of Hull. Professor Johnston has researched extensively in the areas of reading disorders and reading development. She received an MBE for services to education in the 2012 New Year Honours list.

The authors have together investigated the teaching of reading with beginning readers for the past 18 years. These studies have been reported in Johnston, R.S. and Watson, J. (2004), 'Accelerating the development of reading, spelling and phonemic awareness', Reading and Writing, 17 (4), 327-357; Johnston, R.S. and Watson, J.E. (2006), 'The effectiveness of synthetic phonics teaching in developing reading and spelling skills in English speaking boys and girls', in Joshi, R.M., and Aaron, P.G. (Eds), *Handbook of Orthography and Literacy*, LEA: London; Johnston, R.S., Watson, J.E., and Logan, S. (2009), 'Enhancing word reading, spelling and reading comprehension skills with synthetic phonics teaching: studies in Scotland and England', in Wood, C. and Connelly, V., *Contemporary Perspectives on Reading and Spelling*, Routledge, London.

There are also a number of reports for the Scottish government: 'Accelerating reading attainment: the effectiveness of synthetic phonics', *Interchange 57* (SOEID, 1998), 'Accelerating reading and spelling with synthetic phonics: A five year follow up', *Insight 4* (SEED, 2003), 'A seven year study of the effects of synthetic phonics teaching on reading and spelling attainment', *Insight 17* (SEED, 2005) and 'The effects of synthetic phonics teaching on reading and spelling attainment: a seven year longitudinal study' (The Scottish Executive Central Research Unit, 2005), available at <http://www.scotland.gov.uk/library5/education/sptrs-00.asp>.